Brighter Freedom

A Journey from Broken to Brighter

Cindy Rahm

Dedication

This Is for You!

To find the courage to take another step
To find healing for your soul
To build a life of freedom
To build a brighter life

Lord, bless these readers with the courage to overcome their
brokenness. Give them ears to hear your voice for directions, eyes
to see the next steps, and hearts that love you more and more
through the process. We praise you in advance for the miracles
and joy that are coming. ~ *In Jesus' name. Amen.*

Contents

Be Free

Then Jesus said to those Jews who believed Him, "If you abide in My word, you are My disciples indeed. And you shall know the truth, and the truth shall make you free."
John 8:31–32

Lord God, I pray for every reader of this book to be filled with new awe of you and learn to abide in you in a fresh way. Your Word is our path to freedom. It contains everything we need for a life of freedom. Give all of us the eye-opening, heart-changing, sweet song of freedom that comes from you alone. Teach us to rejoice so that we will be brighter lights to those around us. *~In the precious name of Jesus, I pray. Amen.*

Introductions

Meet Nehemiah

To set the stage, let's look at some ancient history of the Middle East. Nebuchadnezzar was a great king of Persia who ruled Babylon (now known as Iraq) from about 605 BC–562 BC[1]. During his reign, Nebuchadnezzar captured most of the people and exiled them from their homeland when he invaded Israel. Forced relocation was a customary practice of war to dilute a captured population's loyalties, culture, religion, and family ties. Jerusalem was in ruins after the invasion, including the wall that previously surrounded and protected the city. In those days, a city without a guarded wall was the target of bandits, wild animals, and invasions. Over time, another king, Cyrus, permitted some Israelites to return to Jerusalem and rebuild the temple, but most of the city was still in ruins and unprotected.

Our story begins around 445 BC, during the reign of Babylonian King Artaxerxes I[2]. We meet our hero, Nehemiah (nee-uh-my-uh), who held the trusted position of the king's cupbearer. Nehemiah was of Jewish heritage, had a heart for his ancestry, and had faith in God. His story is an example of determination and leadership because of how he rallied the oppressed Jewish people to rebuild the wall around the city from all the ruins left in Jerusalem.

Meet Cindy

I was like the strong wall around Jerusalem, a mighty fortress capable of protecting my inner self from the world and all its hurts.

I thought I could withstand anything because I loved God and was intelligent, creative, and confident.

In my fifties, my life dramatically changed because of several significant life events, starting with the breakup of my twenty-two-year marriage. That led me to accept that my drinking was out of control, and I began the Christ-centered journey of sobriety with Celebrate Recovery. This program taught me new concepts and brought me closer to God than I ever imagined. I felt like a new person.

But then...

After a few bad decisions, my world began to crack, crumble, tumble—and then it completely crashed. A traumatic remarriage, involvement in a church that turned out to be a cult, and financial disaster destroyed me emotionally. And then, it got worse. Ultimately, I became a broken pile of tears and just a shadow of my former self. My walls of strength had crumbled into ruins.

I was now facing difficult choices: I could swirl in the gloom as a victim or rebuild and restore. Based on the title of this book, you may have figured out that I chose the path of restoration to become better than I was before.

Meet Brokenness

Brokenness can come from our internal struggles with unmet needs and unhealed hurts. Your brokenness may be due to any of the following: grief, abuse, addiction, trauma, financial disaster, shame, betrayal, anger, worry, family dysfunction, loneliness, regret, mental illness, self-hatred, toxic relationships, unbearable temptations, fear, anxiety, confusion, or many other sources.

Thankfully, God is a healer of all these and more. He can help us go from a broken pile of rubble to a robust and mature warrior for Jesus, standing every day against the battles of this world. As you read, I hope you will find many valuable nuggets of gold in the piles of rubble from which you are emerging.

Meet Freedom

What is freedom? Freedom comes when we are so firmly rooted in our relationship with God that the inevitable storms and damage of the world no longer destroy us. They no longer send us reeling in fear or self-protection. They don't take over our reactions the way they used to. We are free to take a breath and ask for guidance from the Holy Spirit because he is our helper (John 14:26). Freedom comes when we abide in God and weave him into our day-to-day reactions.

How does someone get to freedom? Everyone has a different journey, and this book is a vulnerable look at some of what I went through to learn about freedom. These chapters will also present practical ways to incorporate freedom into *your* journey. I won't just talk about my mess. I want to show how, as they say, to "turn the mess into a message." I will include points that can help you gain freedom too.

It may not seem obvious how my story corresponds with the biblical story of Nehemiah. Nehemiah started with a pile of rubble, and so did I. Nehemiah rebuilt the wall around Jerusalem, while I rebuilt my life by building a pathway to freedom. We both relied on God to do what we didn't think could be done.

I saw a few choices as I contemplated my pile of rubble:

- I could walk away from God and enjoy the world.

- I could embrace my despair and victim mentality.

- I could overcome destruction and find the freedom Jesus promised us.

To use Nehemiah metaphors the choices would be:

- I could stay in Babylon and live for pleasure.

- I could live in Jerusalem's piles of rubble.

- I could rebuild the wall and the gates.

I chose victory and rejoicing instead of the rubble. I decided to rebuild a path to freedom, not walls that only provide a temporary illusion of strength and protection.

You have a choice too.

The path to freedom runs straight through the garden of Gethsemane, where Jesus committed himself to the next steps of his ministry: death, burial, and resurrection. In the same way, I committed to my next steps:

- death to my old ways of approaching life

- burial of my old ways, covering them with the Word of God

- resurrection as an overcomer filled with the breath of the Holy Spirit and led by his love

I acknowledge that I still have a long way to go, but this is my journey so far.

Meet This Book

Each chapter has two sections. Chapters begin with a Bible reference from Nehemiah's historical account from which we will develop a metaphorical boulder as the topic for that chapter. Then, using that spiritual principle, we will also look at how the New Testament can help us walk out of our current wreckage. I will apply that principle to some facets of my healing journey to show how you can do it too. You may be surprised that the wisdom found in Nehemiah still applies today, 2600 years later.

Why fifty-two chapters? Once Nehemiah arrived back in Jerusalem and convinced the people to help rebuild the city wall, they did all the work in *fifty-two* days. So, we will walk sequentially through the book of Nehemiah to see what spiritual treasures we can find for our freedom journey to build a path out of our wreckage.

In these chapters, we will learn more ways to pull out the bitter roots of our past, stop fearing the future, and abide in Jesus more fully in the present. We will learn to re-joy and sometimes even to rejoice.

Rubble

When Life Falls Apart

Brighter Freedom

Chapter 1

Broken

And they said to me,
"The remnant there in the province who survived the captivity are in great distress and disgrace, and the wall of Jerusalem is broken down and its gates have been burned with fire."
Nehemiah 1:3

Long before our story begins, Babylon's King Nebuchadnezzar invaded Israel, destroying Jerusalem and the wall around the city. He captured most of the citizens, exiling them to Babylon in Persia. Over time, different Babylonian kings ruled the territory of Israel, and eventually, many Jews were allowed to return. This group was considered a remnant of the original nation. The Israelites received permission to rebuild the temple of God in Jerusalem, but much of the city was still in ruins.

The biblical account of Nehemiah begins around 445 BC during the reign of the Persian King Artaxerxes I. Nehemiah was of Jewish heritage and was born in Babylon, but he still considered Israel his homeland. This story is a historical account of events, and we find Nehemiah living as a servant in the Persian palace when he learns about the distressed condition of Jerusalem, the city of his ancestors and heritage.

In ancient times, city walls were essential to keep out wild animals and enemies. Walls provided strength and security, but an enemy's ultimate strike was tearing down the city walls during an invasion. As a result, those communities became vulnerable to other attacks. A city with broken-down walls was dangerous, so Nehemiah's heart began to ache for the people back in his homeland.

There was no protection or hope for a city with broken walls.

I understand brokenness.

At fifty-eight years old, I reached a state of personal brokenness and hopelessness. I never imagined I could experience the depth of hurt, fear, rejection, confusion, and despair that I found myself in. Like the walls of Jerusalem, my life was like a pile of rubble surrounding a frail and fearful core. By the time I became that broken pile of rubble, I had already been through some profound, life-defining lessons.

I got married in my early twenties, but things changed quickly after he became addicted to prescription painkillers. When his source of drugs ran out, he started using heroin on the streets, and that person I loved disappeared. Suddenly, his activities included mysterious behavior, stealing, needles, chaos, and even guns. After a few failed attempts at treatment programs, divorce became necessary to protect myself.

I needed a normal life, and I married a great guy at the age of thirty. I wanted to raise a family with this man and grow old together. We followed the typical middle-class, Midwestern American dream—held professional jobs, attended church, and raised two sons. However, we also adopted unhealthy ways of dealing with the stresses of life until the marriage I thought would last forever ended in divorce after twenty-two years.

After acknowledging my drinking had spiraled out of control, I chose to get sober and put an end to that coping mechanism. At that point, I felt I had lived through a reasonable number of troubles for one lifetime and imagined I would be entering my golden years with strength, security, and satisfaction. Unfortunately, the worst was yet to come.

Without warning, I came under attack, an invasion. I suddenly found myself in a spiritual war that caught me off guard. Interestingly, in spiritual warfare, we often become our own enemies. Spiritual warfare can include being deceived and drawn into making wrong choices. I was naive and made some horrible financial, career, and relationship decisions.

I fell for some sweet-sounding promises and opened the wrong doors. The mix of those decisions created a perfect storm. I remarried at the age of fifty-five and entered what I call my dark years. The relationship was traumatic, to say the least. I quickly found myself in a sexually, emotionally, and spiritually abusive situation. I moved with my new spouse across the country to an unfamiliar area where I had no acquaintances except for some of his family. We became involved—excitedly at first—in a long-distance church arrangement with a small congregation in Israel. However, the more we engaged with this church, the more we recognized its unsound, cult-like teachings and controlling leaders. I was now living with multiple kinds of abuse from my spouse *and* my church. I was trying to hide and yet trying to call out for help at the same time.

This short but harsh marriage and cult completely wrecked me. My circumstances had me trapped, and I needed to escape. Then, suddenly, everything collapsed around me, leaving me nowhere to turn. I was completely isolated, with no husband, money, friends, or church family to lean on. To make matters worse, I lost the job that was my only chance of achieving stability. Every aspect of my life was shattered—family, career, spirituality, home, friendships, finances, and even another marriage.

So, there I was: broken.

So, if you think you are standing firm, be careful that you don't fall!
1 Corinthians 10:12 NIV

Lord, you love us even when we fall, even when we make mistakes, even when we don't know what to do next. You will help us pick up the pieces. I pray that those experiencing brokenness will find hope, healing, and freedom as they learn to trust you in new ways. *~Amen.*

Chapter 2

Weeping

> So it was, when I heard these words, that I sat down and wept, and
> mourned for many days; I was fasting and praying before the God of
> heaven... I confess the sins we Israelites, including myself and my father's
> family, have committed against you.
> Nehemiah 1:4, 6 NIV

After he heard about the devastation in Jerusalem, Nehemiah was heartbroken for the people of Israel. While he was living in the comfort of a palace in a foreign land, his kin lived in a rundown city without protection. Nehemiah was brought to his knees in grief for the people he loved.

Despite the influences of the Babylonian culture, Nehemiah held onto the beliefs of his Jewish ancestry. He loved God, so before taking any action, he humbled himself in repentance and sought the Lord for direction.

We see Nehemiah repenting not just for himself but also for the whole nation. The people of Israel had lost their land as a direct result of their sins and disobedience. God had warned them repeatedly that if they continued down their evil path, they would face judgment, lose his protection, and experience disaster. Nehemiah grasped the bigger picture and began interceding for his people.

Nehemiah engaged in traditional mourning rituals, including weeping, praying, and fasting. He confessed and remembered not only God's warnings but also his promises for restoration.

Like Jerusalem, my life was in ruins. Like Nehemiah, I wept over the situation. I cried uncontrollably, overwhelmed by deep despair. I had to lament my life and the awful direction it took. Through this period of mourning, I could finally start seeing clearly. This new spouse and church had done some evil things to me. However, I also saw my role and how I ended up in such a state of desperation and loneliness.

I had made important decisions with blinders on, ignored red flags, and naively expected everything would work out fine. I assumed the people in my life loved me and wanted what was best for me. But I didn't consider all the possibilities. What if they didn't? What if they didn't even know how to love? What if we were not really on the same team? My assumptions led to the worst mistakes of my life. What's more, my finances and career were in shambles. I didn't have the resources to escape or even the confidence to interview for a new job.

So, I did what Nehemiah did. I turned to God and cried out to him. I cried, and prayed, and lamented, and repented, and mourned, and cried some more at the feet of Jesus. The reality of my situation devastated me. I had nothing left, and all I knew was that Jesus was the answer to all my problems.

Standing behind Him at His feet, weeping, she began to wet His feet with her tears, and she wiped them with the hair of her head, and began kissing His feet and anointing them with the perfume.
Luke 7:38

Lord, at points in life, all we have are tears. Thank you for being with us even in the most challenging moments. *~In Jesus' name. Amen.*

Chapter 3

Positioned

"Please, Lord, may Your ear be attentive to the prayer of Your servant
and the prayer of Your servants who delight to revere Your name, and
please make Your servant successful today and grant him mercy before
this man." Now I was the cupbearer to the king.
Nehemiah 1:11

On his own, Nehemiah would never be able to help rebuild the city of Jerusalem because he was just a servant living in a distant land, but he served a powerful and wealthy king. Unfortunately, speaking to a king without an invitation was punishable by death in the ancient world, so Nehemiah needed an opportunity. He had regular access to the king as the royal cupbearer, but conversing with him would still take a miracle and great courage.

Nehemiah is an example of how we should never give up just because our possibilities seem against the odds. Nehemiah was willing to embrace the challenge. An idea, a God-inspired idea, was bubbling up in his heart to help the people of Jerusalem rebuild the wall. This divine inspiration was more powerful than his fears.

In this verse, we can see how Nehemiah was preparing his heart and countenance to take a huge risk. Nehemiah realized that he was just a servant, but it turns out that God loves a servant's heart. He took his need to the Lord and prayed for success and favor. Before taking his idea to the earthly king, Nehemiah presented his requests before his king in heaven.

It takes great courage to speak to a king.

Sometimes, it takes great courage to acknowledge our problems. Brokenness can transform our hearts to the point where we are finally receptive to living God's way, but we must sometimes go through considerable pain before we are ready to surrender everything to the King.

I have been serving in the Christian recovery world for quite some time, and thankfully, I have learned about denial. Denial is when we ignore, minimize, justify, or rationalize our problems, addictions, hurts, negative behaviors, or lifestyles. We can't even acknowledge our issues because they are our blind spots that are obvious to everyone else. Operating in denial, we take on the role of God of our lives as we try to fix and control the circumstances around us, often making things worse.

Many of us try hard to keep everything from falling apart when we need to accept our brokenness, let go, and wake up enough to make changes. Sometimes, we reach the end of our capacity before we can accept the reality of a situation.

At some point, we must come to terms with the fact that we need to change. We call it "hitting your bottom." At that place, we crumble into a pile of rubble. For me, lying flat on the floor in a broken pile of tears was a valuable position. From there, I could recognize the extent of the devastation in my life and the implications of continuing my current path. From there, I could see my desperate need for more of God. From there, I could begin a new trajectory.

When broken, we begin to emerge from denial and find ourselves in an ideal position before the King of Kings. From this place of brokenness, we are humbled enough to see Him, not ourselves, as the solution. This is not a position of weakness but surrender—surrendering everything to the King of the universe. In this surrender, we find hope and relief, knowing we don't have to manage everything alone.

From this perfect position, I could reach out to Jesus, my King, and finally surrender in desperation and brokenness.

Therefore let's approach the throne of grace with confidence,
so that we may receive mercy and find grace
for help at the time of our need.
Hebrews 4:16

Lord, we are grateful for the invitation into your presence, even into the throne room itself. Despite being on your throne, you understand what it's like to be at the bottom of a pile of rubble. We trust that all the answers will come through you because your throne of grace is just the right place for us to be. *~Amen.*

Chapter 4

Sadness of Heart

So the king said to me, "Why is your face sad, though you are not ill? This is nothing but sadness of heart." Then I was very much afraid. And I said to the king, "May the king live forever. Why should my face not be sad when the city, the site of my fathers' tombs, is desolate and its gates have been consumed by fire?"
Nehemiah 2:2–3

The king noticed something unusual, something not quite right: a sadness of heart. When we are depressed and in mourning, everyone around us can see our broken hearts. Nehemiah was just as broken as the city of his ancestors, and he had trouble hiding it. Thankfully, God can use our brokenness.

After seeing Nehemiah's sadness of heart, King Artaxerxes started a conversation with him. The story tells us that Nehemiah had never been sad in the king's presence before, so the king noticed his change of countenance. God strategically placed Nehemiah in the Babylonian palace for this exact purpose. Nehemiah needed a royal conversation to help his homeland. The king was the only hope. He had all the power, influence, wealth, and authority to fix the situation. Artaxerxes could provide everything necessary to repair the wall and restore the city.

I had a sad heart when I was at the bottom of my pit of despair. The abuse had broken my heart, and I had nowhere to turn. I was living thousands of miles away from my family and friends. I only had one friend in the entire state where I was living, and I had no local church family to support me.

I was afraid to tell anyone what was happening because of fear and shame related to my choices. I blamed myself for everything, and yet I also knew I had suffered some horrible wrongs that had harmed me. In many ways, I was a victim. I hated myself, my life, and my circumstances, and couldn't see any way out. I lived in a very dark place filled with trauma, fear, regret, desperate loneliness, and hopelessness.

Jesus, my king, saw my sadness of heart, and he was there for me.

I could justify my sadness because I had struggled through some complicated problems. Wouldn't anyone be a puddle of tears after living through experiences like this? I was mourning my life, and crying was the only thing I could do. Sure, I was a Christian filled with the Holy Spirit, but this was a life crisis. Jesus saw that, too, and he would soon show me more about how powerful my trust in him could become. But for now, crying was enough.

The righteous cry out, and the LORD hears and rescues them from all their troubles. The LORD is near to the brokenhearted and saves those who are crushed in spirit.
Psalms 34:17–18

God, sometimes our suffering consumes us and brings us to overwhelming despair. But you are always near and love us through the pain of our broken hearts. I pray for those in the middle of brokenness to experience your presence and feel your loving arms wrapped around them. *~Amen.*

Chapter 5

The King

Then the king said to me, "What would you request?" So I prayed to the God of heaven. Then I said to the king, "If it pleases the king, and if your servant has found favor before you, I request that you send me to Judah, to the city of my fathers' tombs, that I may rebuild it." Then the king said to me, with the queen sitting beside him, "How long will your journey be, and when will you return?" So it pleased the king to send me, and I gave him a definite time.
Nehemiah 2:4–6

Nehemiah used his opportunity to request permission to rebuild Jerusalem. As an observer of royal court procedures, he was familiar with the correct approaches for his presentation, and he used that to his advantage. He presented his request with reverence, respect, and humility. Nehemiah gave a sincere and short elevator pitch and communicated his desire to go to Israel to begin a massive rebuilding process—and the king agreed. Pitching with passion, respect, and humility instead of pride and ego can influence a king.

The king knew Nehemiah well enough to put him in charge of a monumental building effort. Such an undertaking would require an organized, forward-thinking, passionate manager who could maneuver through the political roadblocks that are sure to happen on an extensive community civil engineering project. A similar project today would require a business plan and project schedules, risk mitigation plans, and materials lists with price quotes. Yet somehow, Nehemiah got the buy-in he needed with simple, humble requests.

That could only happen if God were on his side.

I have a King. This King knows me personally and even calls me by my name. He lets me sit in his lap, sobbing, while he holds and rocks me, even when I have a sloppy, crying face with red eyes and a runny nose. He comforts me in my despair because this King is also my caring daddy.

I did not have a good biological daddy. He was never around much and was an alcoholic who was always fighting with my mom. He completely abandoned the family during my teen years. He died after we briefly reconciled when I was in my early twenties. Consequently, I have always struggled to think of God as a father—I didn't know what a healthy fatherly relationship was like.

Seeing God as a distant king was more natural for me. Even during that traumatic season of destruction, God was my biggest priority, yet I still couldn't come to him as a loving daddy. That kind of persona for God never resonated with me. It wasn't my reality. God was King on the throne, but he was not my devoted Papa.

In the past, when I suffered, I stuffed it with false comforts like alcohol or a vacation or overloaded myself with projects and accomplishments. But I couldn't do that this time—the destruction was too complete, and I didn't know where to turn.

My way out had to include coming to terms with the fact that I am a child of the King. God, the King of Kings, has adopted me into his family and hears me when I am crying. He knew my heart and needs but let me cry out to him anyway.

At this point, I could not do anything myself and needed God's help to start over. I needed to rebuild my entire life. So, I cried out, "God, Abba Father, help me! I can't do it, and since you are a good Father, a King, *my* King, I come to you for help."

I just had to trust that he was the only way out of my suffering.

The Spirit you received brought about your adoption to sonship. And by him we cry, "Abba, Father." The Spirit himself testifies with our spirit that we are God's children. Now if we are children, then we are heirs—heirs of God and co-heirs with Christ, if indeed we share in his sufferings in order that we may also share in his glory.
Romans 8:15–17 NIV

Father God, you are our Abba Daddy in heaven. You chose us, adopted us, and became the loving Father we need. You are not only a Father but also the King of Kings and Creator of the universe. And we are coheirs to all you have. Thank you! *~Amen.*

Chapter 6

More, Please!

And I said to the king, "If it pleases the king, let letters be given me for the
governors of the provinces beyond the River, so that they will allow me
to pass through until I come to Judah, and a letter to Asaph the keeper
of the king's forest, so that he will give me timber to make beams for the
gates of the citadel which is by the temple, for the wall of the city, and for
the house to which I will go." And the king granted them to me because
the good hand of my God was on me.
Nehemiah 2:7–8

In ancient times, the perils of travel were immense, and people needed to make extensive preparations before embarking on
journeys. According to a Google query, the distance from Babylon
to Jerusalem, though seemingly short at five hundred miles as the
crow flies, was, in reality, a nine-hundred-mile trip, depending on
the actual route[1]. The journey was not just about the destination
but also about survival along the way. In addition to all the building
supplies, they would have also brought several weeks' worth of
food, water, and camping supplies. The limited availability of meat
and dairy along the road would have required bringing live animals
and grain to feed them. That means their pace was only as fast as
the animals could travel. A traveling party would also need guards
for protection from bandits, wild beasts, and other enemies.

Did you notice that Nehemiah asked the king for more building
supplies? King Artaxerxes had already agreed to many provisions,
but he requested an additional load of lumber. I love how he
realized this kind of generosity from the king could only happen
because of God. Nehemiah knew he could not have earned such
favor on his own—this kind of blessing only came from God.

Several months into my remarriage, everything was caving in, and I realized what a massive mistake I had made. An evil agenda was at play, and I was swept up by it. I was trapped and finally understood why many of the abused women I knew stayed in obviously horrible situations. Now I was like them. I was hiding my shame and fear while praying for a miracle. But it was complicated. Looking back, I could see I had made some critical decisions that caused everything to implode. Certain shortcomings in myself contributed to this. The compounded impact of those decisions and weaknesses created the storm that left me destroyed, just like the walls around Jerusalem.

If you are a Bible-believing Christian, then you know an actual enemy is out there who wants to destroy us and our faith. His name is Satan. If you don't believe in demons, evil spirits, or the devil, then you should reread your Bible. It's a reality: We live in a spiritual world. Satan was chasing me down, and it may have looked like he was winning. But in the depths of my hurt and pain, I had a consistent prayer: "God, I need more of you. More, please, I need more."

To my surprise, there actually *was* more. I had been a practicing Christian for over twenty-five years, and no one had ever told me about the power of the Holy Spirit. He had several honorable mentions, but no one discussed baptism in the Holy Spirit. Many churches completely ignore the Holy Spirit, a vital part of the Trinity along with the Father and Jesus, the Son. The Holy Spirit is actively working in hearts everywhere to equip his people with the fullness of who he is. For me, this happened in the middle of my worst times. Jesus filled me with the Holy Spirit right when I needed him the most, and this was a life-changing experience for me.

We need the Holy Spirit to walk out the Christian life. I honestly think that without that fresh infilling of the Holy Spirit, I would have seriously considered suicide. Satan was trying to lead me down that road. But God was leading me upward—into a new awareness of life in the Spirit, which provided the only reason I had any hope left. In my darkest time, I was blessed with a new understanding of the work and role of the Holy Spirit. This new knowledge was an invigorating awakening to all God has for me.

I was finally part of a church that embraced the Holy Spirit, but unfortunately, this church also twisted certain aspects of Scripture. Eventually, I even realized that it was a cult. I was simultaneously being bombarded with fresh truths and damaging lies. I was personally experiencing exponential spiritual growth with this filling of the Holy Spirit, but I was confused and concerned about many concepts they were teaching. Thankfully, God was very gracious and protected me in so many ways.

I couldn't discard this good from God just because some people were off track in how they used it. Eliminating or ignoring the gifts of the Spirit is just as wrong as misusing them. Some readers might disagree, and that's okay, but I believe that failure to recognize manifestations of the Holy Spirit today is just as unhealthy to the body of Christ as misusing the gifts. I have genuinely experienced these gifts and cannot deny their reality. Especially praying in tongues, which gave new hope and encouragement to my entire being.

One thing is sure: Walking with the Holy Spirit helps us in all spiritual warfare. God gave me more tools, insight, and goodness to help me through the confusion and abuse. Yes, I discovered there was much more to the Christian life than I was aware of. Now, I had to prepare myself to walk in it correctly and discern the truth. My rebuilding process has included a better understanding of the Holy Spirit. He really does have more for us.

"So I say to you, ask, and it will be given to you; seek, and you will find; knock, and it will be opened to you... "So if you, despite being evil, know how to give good gifts to your children, how much more will your heavenly Father give the Holy Spirit to those who ask Him?"
Luke 11:9, 13

Thank you. Lord, for opening my eyes to all that you are and all that you have for us. I pray for every reader to want more of what you have for them: more of your gifts, more of your wisdom, more of your Spirit. Thank you that you are a good Father who lavishes your own Spirit on those who ask for it. *~In Jesus' name, we pray. Amen.*

Chapter 7

Go!

So I went to Jerusalem.
Nehemiah 2:11 NIV

King Artaxerxes provided Nehemiah with all the necessary resources to embark on his mission, leading him to Jerusalem, a city of historical and religious importance. Jerusalem had seen ongoing conflict and turmoil and experienced many cycles of destruction and reconstruction. What distinguishes this particular narrative of rebuilding is the role of an ordinary man, Nehemiah, who returned to his homeland to unite the community in a project that would benefit all.

The people of Jerusalem weren't aware of Nehemiah's plans when he first rolled into town, but something good was about to happen. Everyone needed the protection of the city walls, but the community didn't have a leader to organize the effort to fix the problem. The people became complacent about living alongside the debris. They tolerated the tension and fear that comes with being unprotected. It became their normal.

Nehemiah had a heart of compassion for his people, and the people needed someone to help them rise above their current circumstances, so it was a perfect match. Although the king commissioned Nehemiah to go to Jerusalem to build up the walls physically, God commissioned him to build up the people emotionally and spiritually. Nehemiah was about to transform the entire city by taking a broken culture, giving it purpose, and bringing a spiritual revival.

Nehemiah didn't come to town to be a hero, but he did come there to be a champion.

But what was I going to do? I couldn't continue like this. The abusive marriage I entered four years prior was one of my life's vast piles of wreckage. After disentangling from the cultish church, I found trustworthy, godly counsel, and God graciously released me from the horrible situation. I was encouraged to move into a new season of life—a season of healing. God was setting me up for something I hadn't seen in a while: hope.

Now what? Where would I go? My brother offered to let me come live with his family for a few months while I figured out what to do next. We had not lived in the same state since he joined the Navy at eighteen, so this would be interesting.

The move was ten hours from where I lived, so I packed what I could to start life over and fit everything into a small U-Haul trailer. On my fifty-ninth birthday, I started life over. As I drove away, my memories returned to the suburban life I had lived for twenty-some years. Now, all I had were these remnants stuffed into a small trailer. Over the years, I had downsized, but this was drastically shedding my belongings. I mourned because I had to let go of possessions I thought of as treasures and important items.

I was lightening my load, but it was hard because I used to have so much stuff. Back in the day, while my kids were growing up, we had a big house and nice vacations, happy family Christmas pictures, kitchen gadgets, and bins of seasonal decorations. Things. Stuff. Now, those possessions were gone and just part of the past. I wanted those things but didn't need them.

Salvation is like that. We receive a new spirit and come alive spiritually, but we still want to carry our old baggage. When I got saved, I became an entirely new creation, so I didn't *need* all the excess baggage anymore: the striving for recognition, the desire to run the show, and the need for status, wealth, instant gratification, and those shiny possessions. My worldly values became extra baggage, but I let those strivings continue to motivate and comfort me for too long. I chose to carry those burdens and carnal desires around, but I would have been better off without them. I thought that was my identity, but they defined my old ways and not what I needed for the new kingdom life. Living in the kingdom, we get to replace our old worldly values, wants, and desires with true, lasting, and loving ones. Until I was broken, I didn't realize they were unnecessary.

I drove away, leaving behind the old worldly treasures. The winding roads would take me to new places. I was moving forward into a new life led by the Holy Spirit with treasures that cannot be bought. I recommitted to being a new creation.

The treasure of being a new creation in Christ was better than anything I could see in the rearview mirror.

Therefore if anyone is in Christ, this person is a new creation; the old things passed away; behold, new things have come.
2 Corinthians 5:17

Lord, this freedom journey will take all of us to new places and help form us into the new creation we were destined to be. We can only do that by letting go of the past and traveling with you down the path to a bright new future. Glory to God! *~Amen.*

Chapter 8

Scope It Out

After dark I went out through the Valley Gate, past the Jackal's Well, and
over to the Dung Gate to inspect the broken walls and burned gates.
Then I went to the Fountain Gate and to the King's Pool, but my donkey
couldn't get through the rubble.
Nehemiah 2:13–14 NLT

After being in Jerusalem for a few days, Nehemiah decided it was time to scope out the project. He still had not gone public with his plans to rebuild the wall and its gates, so his reconnaissance mission was undercover at night. Nehemiah's inspection confirmed that the wall was merely piles of rubble in many spots, which was ineffective for keeping the city safe.

After seeing the state of the wall firsthand, Nehemiah could now prepare a more specific plan. Ten massive gates had to be rebuilt, and miles of wall had to be reconstructed from the existing rubble. However, many sections and towers were still intact and did not require rebuilding. As a side note, the wall has been demolished and rebuilt again since Nehemiah. Today's wall is over eight feet wide, forty feet tall, and two and a half miles long, which can help us appreciate the scope of the work involved.

The next step for Nehemiah was to market the idea to the people targeted to do the work. Everyone living in Jerusalem would have to help as laborers until the job was complete, so they all needed to make a significant commitment. With the scope of the project in mind, Nehemiah could now develop a campaign and plan to rally everyone to cooperate.

My problems were overwhelming, and my repeated failures had left me with no confidence in my ability to dig out of my current dilemma. As I scoped out my situation, I had some huge issues to overcome:

- emotional health: wrecked

- spiritual health: wrecked

- relationships: wrecked

- self-image: wrecked

- marriage: wrecked

- finances: wrecked

- home: wrecked

Embracing that list meant accepting all the negative aspects in my life. They were facts, but that didn't mean I had to embrace them. It was like the people of Jerusalem living for decades with the rubble of the fallen wall and never doing anything about it. They couldn't overcome it by themselves, and neither could I. But I have a big God. Then I realized a truth of game-changing significance: God loves me despite my long list of failures. That list may be full of facts, but my God is full of hope.

I started my journey of rebuilding by learning about my identity in Christ. Even though my life was wrecked, some fantastic promises were true, no matter what negative things were happening. These promises had to be scoped out so I could see the whole picture.

- I am loved by Jesus (John 15:9)

- I have the mind of Christ (1 Corinthians 2:16)

- I am a temple filled with the Holy Spirit (1 Corinthians 3:16)

- I can do all things through Christ who strengthens me (Philippians 4:13)

- The one who is in me is greater than the one who is in the world (1 John 4:4)

- I am not alone (Matthew 28:20)

- I am his friend (John 15:15)

Wow! I had more going for me than I knew and more than I first believed. I knew the Bible. I had read these truths before, and they lived somewhere in my head, but I didn't believe them in my heart.

I learned that we could paraphrase, personalize verses, and declare them over ourselves. Then I learned that if we say verses out loud, our soul hears the truth about who we are, so we will learn to believe it. We can learn new truths when we repeatedly hear them. Through the scientific concept of neuroplasticity, we can rewire our brains to destroy negative self-concepts and believe in God's promises instead. We can reprogram our negative thinking patterns and renew our minds by hearing God's promises (saying them out loud). Look how science supports the Bible!

This is how you form either a negative or positive view of yourself: by hearing and believing. If you constantly hear or tell yourself that you are ugly, dumb, unlovable, worthless, or whatever, that will form a negative stronghold in your heart. Likewise, if you hear or tell yourself that you are valued, loved, forgiven, and victorious, then you will form a positive stronghold in your heart. It may take a long time, but eventually, we can begin to believe what the Word says about us.

My experiences may say that I'm unlovable, unsuccessful, ugly, and alone. But as a Christian, I am loved, provided for, and an overcomer. And Jesus says I am his friend.

Therefore, I say to you, all things for which you pray and ask, believe that you have received them, and they will be granted to you.
Mark 11:24

Lord Jesus, our friend, you tell us to pray confidently, believing our prayers are heard and answered. Your Word is for us and gives us our very identity when we believe what it says. ~*Amen.*

Chapter 9

Wake Up

**Then I said to them,
"You see the bad situation we are in, that Jerusalem is desolate and its
gates have been burned by fire. Come, let's rebuild the wall of Jerusalem
so that we will no longer be a disgrace."
Nehemiah 2:17**

Nehemiah revealed his plans to the leaders, Jewish priests, and officials of Jerusalem. He already had the needed materials and permission from the king to do the job, so the next step was acquiring laborers willing to do all the hard work. Nehemiah reminded them that their national pride could be restored along with the wall, and their cooperation would ensure success.

The people had grown accustomed to walking around piles of rocks and debris as they went about their business because they had been living in the rubble of the unprotected city for so long. The rubble reminded them of their past defeats, undermining their sense of value and blurring their memories of past blessings and the beautiful experiences of their ancestors.

Nehemiah came on the scene with grand plans, high hopes, deep pockets, and the authority to make changes that could radically improve their existence. He had everything they needed to get the job done. Now, Nehemiah's biggest challenge was encouraging the people and helping them adjust their attitude. They needed to break through the walls of denial and stop walking around in piles of debris.

Initially, I was blind to all the wreckage I had to deal with. I had built up walls of pride to protect me from verbal assaults, walls of indifference to keep me safe from inevitable abandonment, and walls of sarcasm to deflect my insecurities. I started waking up to how those coping and protection mechanisms kept me safe for a while, but eventually, they hardened my heart. Then, when real trauma slammed into them, these walls crumbled completely, and I became a victim.

As we survey the mess from past trauma, we can easily assume we will keep living with the mess, thinking, *I'll never get over this*, *I can't forgive them*, or *that experience defines me*. This kind of thinking keeps us stuck in a rut and causes us to embrace the role of a victim. These self-defeating statements are a type of vow that creates strongholds defining our identity. We embrace victimization if we don't wake up to the impact of our thoughts and words.

That's what happened to me. I couldn't see my victim mentality because I was so overwhelmed with justifiable hurt. I felt the weight of every brick of my broken walls piled on top of me. It was easier to lie under the pile of rubble than to start pulling off the bricks, but I knew God had a better purpose for me. He didn't want me to stay stuck. He wanted me to take the bricks, one at a time, and lay them down to build that road forward so I could crush my enemy, the devil, under my feet. My road forward was going to be built on truth instead of fear. I was about to transform walls into roads—what a concept.

That road construction has been going on for several years, but I started the rubble-removal process with just one brick. I looked at one of those lies weighing me down and said, "No!" I rejected it and said, "I will get over this!" Then, I repented for believing the lie. Repenting generally means having remorse, being sorry, and changing our minds about what we did wrong. We repent for believing the lies because they take our trust away from God.

Then, I asked God to show me the truth.

The first step to freedom is waking up to the lies we are believing. Sometimes, you can't see the lies because a veil of denial still covers them. Ask God to show you a lie that you believe. Then, ask him to tell you *his* truth about that situation. One of the roles of the Holy Spirit is to reveal God's truth to you, and he will do it if you ask him. This is how God helps us do what we can't do on our own. He comes in with a wake-up call, revealing one lie at a time, the one thing we can handle today. Then, he gives us one truth to replace it. Jesus is the truth that replaces the lies.

I was becoming a bricklayer. Jesus must be the first brick—the all-important cornerstone that holds the new road in place. God the Father is the architect who designs the path of the new road, and the Holy Spirit is the mortar that binds all the parts together.

Jesus is "'the stone you builders rejected, which has become the cornerstone.' Salvation is found in no one else, for there is no other name under heaven given to mankind by which we must be saved."
Acts 4:11–12 NIV

God, thank you for helping us wake up to the truth that you are the cornerstone of our progress. Holy Spirit, show me the lies I have believed about myself so I can wake up. What is the truth that I need to know today? *~Amen.*

Rebuilding

Peace by Piece

Brighter Freedom

Chapter 10

Yes

And I told them of the hand of my God which had been good upon me,
and also of the king's words that he had spoken to me.
So they said, "Let us rise up and build."
Then they set their hands to this good work.
Nehemiah 2:18 NKJV

One yes leads to another. After God gave him the grandiose idea to rebuild the walls of Jerusalem, Nehemiah immediately responded with his yes, and the rest is truly history. This small yes to God was not just a mere agreement but a powerful seed God used to pave the way for his next step, stirring the heart of King Artaxerxes, who also said yes. Then, the king gave Nehemiah all the supplies, funding, and authority needed for the rebuilding project. This shows the cascading power of a single yes. But still, another yes was required.

As God's plan continued to unfold, Nehemiah's words and Artaxerxes's provisions stirred the hearts of the citizens. In a remarkable display of unity and shared vision, they, too, responded with a yes and committed to action. Their willingness to become the laborers needed to rebuild the wall was not just a commitment to a physical task but a testament to their faith and trust in God's plan.

Nehemiah's leadership was instrumental in gaining the approval of the people of Jerusalem for the rebuilding project. His ability to generate enthusiasm and inspire the people to embrace this civic endeavor was remarkable. This kind of project in the ancient world would have required thousands of hours of hard labor. But the harvest promised to be great. The city would be cleaned up and its honor restored. The wall would provide everyone with the protection they needed.

It was good work, and the people said yes.

Building my road forward and rebuilding my life would be challenging and transformative work. Each step I took was a conscious choice to say yes to the path of freedom and alignment with God. Though this journey required thousands of steps, it promised a bountiful harvest. It was a testament to the power of embracing challenging work as a path to spiritual growth and alignment with God.

Jesus would be at the center of every step forward in my journey. I wanted to be led by the Holy Spirit, which would not necessarily resemble what the world would do. My goal was to make a daily, conscious commitment to conquer the devastation and be an overcomer as God intended. I would say yes to new methods of support, new communities, new churches, and new friendships. I needed new thought processes, jobs, homes, and priorities. This was not just a step, but a seed sown for a future harvest. I could look forward to embracing my rebuilding process with faith and determination because the transformation was coming.

I committed to doing whatever it took, which meant some areas of my life needed to die and then be rebuilt. When seeds go into the ground, their old structure dies as they germinate and sprout into new growth. I had to do that too. I let some things in my life die to become firmly rooted in God's ways and grow into the person he wanted me to be.

Each of the bricks I put under my feet represented a victory over an area of my earlier misery, creating a road away from the mess. The yes seeds I sowed were all my hurts. Each one had to die and be buried. Only then could they grow into useful plants that reap fruitful little harvests in their own time—harvests of new perspectives, peace, and maturity.

That is how it works in God's garden.

When you put a seed into the ground, it doesn't grow into a plant unless it
dies first. And what you put in the ground is not the plant that will grow,
but only a bare seed of wheat or whatever you are planting. Then God
gives it the new body he wants it to have. A different plant grows from
each kind of seed.
1 Corinthians 15:36–38 NLT

Lord God, we give you our yes and are thankful we can put our
old life to death and grow into a unique plant in your kingdom.
~Amen.

Chapter 11

Enemy Attacks

But when Sanballat the Horonite and Tobiah the Ammonite official, and
Geshem the Arab heard about it, they mocked us and despised us, and
said, "What is this thing that you are doing?
Are you rebelling against the king?"
Nehemiah 2:19

Just as the people of Jerusalem were getting excited about the
rebuilding project, opposition from the hostile neighbors began.
Every great idea has opposition, so that's not surprising. The
officials, obviously uninformed, started ridiculing and mocking
Nehemiah and then brought a surprise accusation against him:
rebellion.

Generally, constructive challenges to our ideas are healthy because they bring visibility to gaps and mistakes in our thinking.
Some challengers even help us transform good ideas into great
ideas.

Then, there are malicious attackers, enemies who want to poison others against you. Nehemiah was facing poison in this attack.
These three men were outsiders and didn't want to see the Jewish
people succeed, so they immediately started planting negative
thoughts of fear and doubt throughout the city. They tried to
turn the people against Nehemiah's plans and derail the project
altogether. They intended to keep Jerusalem weak and unsecured
and to keep the people discouraged through intimidation and
bullying.

This kind of enemy tries to stir up trouble. They had no desire
for Nehemiah to be a successful leader. Could there be a more
extensive agenda at play? Was it just those three people, or was

this attack even broader than that? The Bible reminds us that our true enemy works *through* people, and our battles are ultimately fought in the spiritual realm, often fighting for territories here on earth. It is not surprising that enemies would show up for this rebuilding project.

My biggest enemy was in my head, and sometimes, the attacks were fierce. I would hear the lies in my thoughts, telling me that God didn't love me anymore because of what I had done to keep myself safe. As I started working on my new road to freedom, those thoughts constantly tormented me. I was all alone and felt like I would never be normal again because I didn't fit in anywhere. So many people had alienated and abandoned me. I felt there was no hope for someone like me because I had ruined my life and any chance of a healthy marriage. Fear, doubt, and condemnation were constantly yelling at me as plainly as those guys had yelled at Nehemiah.

The past wanted to keep me in its grip. That's how the enemy of our souls works. He keeps us focused on the defeats of our past and makes us constantly feel like victims. Satan keeps us oppressed by feeding negativity into our thoughts and reminding us of our mistakes, problems, and traumas.

During the worst part of my abuse, I experienced a frightening and extreme attack that continued to haunt me for a long time. A demonic face appeared, laughing and announcing that I belonged to him—he owned me. This face was an actual, authentic experience, but it was also a symbolic vision of the depth of the spiritual attack I was under. My response was to become numb to what was happening so I could endure. I was grieved to my core, and I wanted to die. I became an easy target for the enemy's taunts as new doors to torment were opened.

Most attacks are not so openly demonic. Satan finds an opportunity to harass us through abuse, curses, generational issues, occult and New Age activities, drugs and addictions, ungodly sexual activity, and any kind of sinful behavior. These activities open doors to demonic harassment. Yes, even when we are naive and don't understand the implications of our actions, we can bring on new levels of torment. Evil spirits (a.k.a. demons or fallen angels) can oppress Christians and non-Christians alike, meaning we can be tormented and harassed.

Harassment can be as simple as having a bad day or as big as having a series of devastating life events. Harassment can include being bombarded with temptations or illnesses. Torment can also be the inability to get thoughts out of your head; it can drive procrastination on essential tasks or attacks from others, like we see happening to Nehemiah.

There is no biblical support for the possession of a Christian by a demon or evil spirit, but you can be attacked by forces from the dark side. Possession is when demonic entities take over your spirit, which cannot happen to a Christian because the Holy Spirit has already filled that territory. Oppression, however, is harassment by demonic entities in your body or soul but not in your spirit. Oppression and harassment happen to everyone to some degree.

Like Nehemiah, we must be ready for enemy attacks during our time of rebuilding. Thankfully, God knew these attacks would happen and offered guidance so we would not be defenseless.

Put on the full armor of God, so that you can take your stand against the devil's schemes. For our struggle is not against flesh and blood, but against the rulers, against the authorities, against the powers of this dark world and against the spiritual forces of evil in the heavenly realms. Therefore put on the full armor of God, so that when the day of evil comes, you may be able to stand your ground, and after you have done everything, to stand.
Ephesians 6:11–13 NIV

Jesus, you didn't promise the road to freedom would be easy. I pray that every reader recognizes that the spiritual realm around us contains enemies who want to derail our freedom journey. Prepare us for the battle ahead with the spiritual ammunition we need. *~Amen.*

Chapter 12

Truth and Authority

So I answered them and said to them, "The God of heaven will make us successful; therefore we His servants will arise and build, but you have no part, right, or memorial in Jerusalem."
Nehemiah 2:20

When faced with attacks, we can follow the example of our role model, Nehemiah. He didn't react hastily. Instead, he sought the truth and realized that the root of the problem was not personal but a broader opposition to Israel's success. This understanding guided his response as he confidently proclaimed that God initiated the project and would ensure its success.

The king had personally commissioned Nehemiah to oversee the rebuilding of Jerusalem's walls. Because Nehemiah had all the formal authority needed to carry out his task, he could operate in full confidence despite the enemy's taunts.

When we experience verbal attacks, we naturally feel wounded, so our defense mechanisms kick into action and fire up our pride, anger, and insecurities. When we don't take criticism well, we tend to respond in ways that result in arguments, offense, resentments, unforgiveness, bad decisions, and potentially even burned bridges. To grow in Christian maturity, we should consider how we respond to life challenges.

God is always at the center of truth. Our enemies can attack, but God's truth is always a mighty offensive weapon we can use confidently.

When the heaviest attacks came, I felt like a human target that Satan used to run up his side of the scoreboard. The Bible describes these attacks as "flaming arrows" or "fiery darts" shot by the evil one. One after another, they flew at me. Sometimes, the stings were so intense that I would spiral into obsessive thoughts about what just happened or what might happen. Fear would take over, and I couldn't think of anything else.

Satan's ploys crippled me for years and brought me down. Thankfully, when I started to learn about the importance of knowing and embracing God's Word in my heart, his Word became my identity. I accepted that when a relationship with God becomes the core of who you are, you can persevere through the storms.

Jesus modeled winning the battle over the adversary for us. Satan harassed Jesus right after he fasted for forty days in the desert. Jesus had one strategy for success: He countered all the accusations and temptations Satan threw at him with "It is written..." (Matthew 4; Luke 4). Because Jesus knew his identity, he knew his true authority over the devil. And after his resurrection, Jesus gave us all his identity and authority through the Holy Spirit.

At first, I did not walk confidently in anything. I had to learn how to use my newfound authority. Yes, I had a nice little list that told me about my identity in Christ, but I had to add the next step: Grab onto what God says about me in Scripture to counter the enemy attacks and lies with the truth. So, I added to my list of declarations.

- I am victorious (Psalm 20:6)

- I am an overcomer (Revelation 12:11)

- I am free (Galatians 5:1)

- I have no fear (Psalm 23:4)

- I am more than a conqueror (Romans 8:37)

- I am forgiven and made clean (1 John 1:9)

- No weapon formed against me will prevail (Isaiah 54:17)

- I am made righteous by the blood of Jesus (Romans 8:4)

- I can do all things through Christ who strengthens me (Philippians 4:1)

- The joy of the Lord is my strength (Nehemiah 8:10)

I needed to ingrain these verses into my soul so I could win the battle—and it helped! Whenever I felt myself spiraling out of control in fear, I would say my list out loud, and peace would come. This peace happens when we step into the truth and authority we have because of our position in Jesus Christ.

I started saying the list multiple times each day to preempt the next attack. It took a long time, but eventually, I started believing that I was who God said I was.

All Scripture is inspired by God and beneficial for teaching, for rebuke, for correction, for training in righteousness; so that the man or woman of God may be fully capable, equipped for every good work.
2 Timothy 3:16–17

Lord, your Word is powerful! It is the foundation of everything we need to navigate the road to freedom successfully. Thank you for your promises, your instruction, and your encouragement. *~In Jesus' name. Amen.*

Chapter 13

First Things First

Eliashib the high priest and his fellow priests went to work and rebuilt the Sheep Gate. They dedicated it and set its doors in place, building as far as the Tower of the Hundred, which they dedicated, and as far as the Tower of Hananel.
Nehemiah 3:1 NIV

The work begins!

We must understand that the first worker Nehemiah commissioned was the high priest, and the first group of laborers appointed were priests. This choice underscores the significance of honoring the Lord in our work. God is honored when we give him the first of anything we receive, accomplish, or own. If we truly trust that he will provide all our needs, we will not hesitate to offer the first part of our income, time, or resources. When we give to God from our first fruits rather than our leftovers, we demonstrate our reliance on him, not ourselves, to ensure we have enough.

Another intriguing aspect of this initial section of repairs is its location along the north end of Jerusalem, close to the temple. Originally, the Sheep Gate was used to bring sheep and other sacrificial animals into the temple for offerings. The Sheep Gate was not just a physical entrance but a symbolic one through which lives were purified and cleansed. Rebuilding this section first also points to the most significant sacrifice yet to come: Jesus, the Lamb of God. Here at the Sheep Gate, the entire project was dedicated.

To properly inventory and evaluate my brokenness, I started with the common denominator in all the problems: me! And the biggest problem was very close to the temple: my heart.

When those metaphorical gates burned down, they left me wide open to enemy attacks, and now I could see the problems they caused. The comforting things of the world did not resolve my root problems, protect me, or give me the love I longed for. Instead, the enemy attacks increased and caused more problems than I already had. My condemnation, shame, hate, and guilt felt out of control, and my broken heart just wanted to be reconciled to God.

As a Christian, the Holy Spirit lives within me, making me his temple. This temple is incompatible with feelings of self-hatred, shame, fear, and guilt. These feelings can keep me from having a close relationship with God in the inner part of the temple, the holy of holies. Hatred keeps us separated from God. I can't hate something God loves, so I had to forgive myself just like God forgave me.

I was willing to do whatever work was needed, so forgiving myself had to be at the top of the list. The process of forgiving myself included being willing to create an inventory and taking it to God. This inventory consisted of the wrongs I have done to others and my sinful responses to what others did to me. A significant step in finding freedom was acknowledging my shortcomings and repenting.

We must lay the entire inventory down at the cross with Jesus. The blood of Jesus washes away sins, and the cross redeems and atones. We can bury all our past in the tomb with Jesus and watch how his resurrection power restores us. We can genuinely have resurrection life on this side of the cross.

Broken gates do not negate our salvation; they just mean we are not the best possible version of ourselves. We can be saved and continue to live in piles of rubble if we choose to, or we can fulfill our destiny with the potential promised. We can repair our broken gates and close doors through repenting, prayer, forgiveness, inner healing, deliverance, and allowing the Holy Spirit to refresh and renew us in every broken area. These methods of spiritual warfare bring healing and freedom that destroy our enemies and allow us to become the overcomers we were meant to be.

Or do you not know that your body is a temple of the Holy Spirit within you, whom you have from God, and that you are not your own? For you have been bought for a price.
1 Corinthians 6:19–20

Lord, your resurrection power lives within us, so we already have the tools to be victorious. Your Holy Spirit will guide us on our path to freedom and help us rebuild the gates that guard our hearts. I pray now for the willingness to go forward. *~Amen.*

Chapter 14

Purpose

Now the sons of Hassenaah built the Fish Gate; they laid its beams
and installed its doors with its bolts and bars. Next to them Meremoth
the son of Uriah the son of Hakkoz made repairs... And next to him
Zadok the son of Baana also made repairs.
Nehemiah 3:3–4

Some guy named Meremoth got his name in the Bible! He
didn't do miracles or change the world, but he was an obedient
servant, and his work is remembered forever. Meremoth had
a purpose, even though it wasn't grandiose. He completed the
job given to him, earning him a place of honor. Millions of
people have read about his contribution. God remembered
Meremoth.

Nehemiah had a purpose, too. He was a project manager
extraordinaire. Although Nehemiah had spent the earlier part
of his life as the king's cupbearer, in this new assignment, God
launched him into his real and true purpose as a leader for the
people of Jerusalem.

Like a good project manager, Nehemiah assigned sections
of the wall to the workers. This book of the Bible records
each section of the wall and each gate repaired. The story also
names many people who worked on the project, reminding
us, 2600 years later, that God pays attention to our detailed
contributions to his kingdom.

Families and neighbors worked side by side on the rebuilding
project, so we can assume that many sections were built simultaneously. Some families worked on sections right in front of their
own homes. Other workers came to help from towns like Jericho,

about an eighteen-mile journey away. Nehemiah showed each person a purpose and a plan to finish the work.

At my regular job, I am a project manager. Maybe that's why I relate to Nehemiah so well. I've always liked what I do for a living, but it's never felt like my purpose. It's noteworthy that Nehemiah's purpose is my vocation, but it's not my purpose. I did not grow up dreaming about how I would organize project tasks in the corporate world. However, I have always known I would be a writer at some point. Writing has been in my heart from an early age, but I never found my voice until recently.

Over the years, I thought I had found purpose many times because I had ideas for new entrepreneurial ways to serve God. I assumed that if it were God-related, it must be my purpose, and he would bless it. I engaged each of these projects in my own strength. By ignoring input from my advisors, I made some terrible decisions that affected me for years, especially financially. In retrospect, I was trying to force my purpose to happen instead of letting it unfold. The good news is that even though I messed it up, God has pulled everything back together.

These last few years have been a time of healing and preparation for the true calling in my life: something new, something involving writing, and something about freedom. I can see now how God was preparing me. I needed to slow down and hear the voice of God. I needed to experience freedom in Christ instead of the Band-Aids the world has to offer. I needed to stop focusing on walls and start building roads. The more I slowed down, the more I transitioned into my real purpose. When it was time, God breathed on my purpose, and it came alive.

As I write these words, I am finally flowing in my purpose.

And we know that all things work together for good to those who love God, to those who are called according to His purpose.
Romans 8:28 NKJV

Lord, you can work through every mistake we make and still use it for your good and your glory. Thank you for redeeming us and using our past to build us for our ultimate purpose. *~Amen.*

Chapter 15

Pride

The next section was repaired by the men of Tekoa, but their nobles would not put their shoulders to the work under their supervisors... the men of Tekoa repaired another section, from the great projecting tower to the wall of Ophel. Nehemiah 3:5, 27 NIV

Nehemiah's project journal mentions a group of men who came to Jerusalem to work on their share of the wall from the town of Tekoa (about twelve miles away). The nobles from this town thought they were too good for manual labor and refused to work. They are the only group who wouldn't participate in the effort, and as to why, most commentaries come to the same conclusion: pride.

Interestingly, the Tekoa folks are the only group mentioned that worked on two separate sections. You wonder if the faithful of Tekoa volunteered for extra work to compensate for their prideful aristocrats. If so, the wrong attitude of a few elites placed an additional load on others.

That's how pride works. It doesn't care about impacting others—it's willingly blind to the problems it causes. Pride seeks entitlement, special treatment, and attention. Pride is rooted in insecurity and fear and leads to both bullying and people-pleasing. Bullying pride manifests as cold-hearted and self-focused while people-pleasing pride manifests more as a codependent fixer of others. Either way, pride seeks its validation from people rather than God.

Pride has undoubtedly been a struggle for me. I had to deal with significant humbling and introspection before I could even acknowledge this character flaw. I mistakenly believed that I was intellectually superior to others. But as I examined my behaviors, decisions, and defense mechanisms, I saw pride seeping in from every corner. It remains an ongoing battle as I continue to peel back more layers. Because pride can be rooted in fear, as I made progress in uncovering pride, I also uncovered more fear. However, I know that humility and focusing on God are the keys to overcoming this issue.

Pride is a spiritual issue that keeps our hearts from accepting all God has for us. I'm not sure if it is theologically correct, but I like to think of the heart as where our soul intersects with our spirit. Imagine your soul (which is your mind, will, and emotions) and your spirit (God's presence in you) as two rivers that merge. You can regulate how much each river flows out of you because the heart reveals what you love and nurture. The Bible even says in John 7:38 (NKJ): "He who believes in Me... out of his heart will flow rivers of living water."

My born-again spirit wants to flow with godliness and love, but I also have unyielded parts of my soul. These aspects of my personality don't want to follow the Jesus program. This part of me flows with worldly attitudes and motivations. These personality traits are stuck in my old ways and still need to be renewed. When I let pride regulate that flow from my heart, my soulish thinking takes over, and I become selfish, cold, and basically a know-it-all. When I let the Holy Spirit be in charge, I flow with God's goodness and love. The more I let the Spirit rule my heart, the more I look like Jesus and the closer to God I feel. I know I'm always close to God, but when pride is in the way, I don't *feel* it.

Focusing on the opposite behavior helps eliminate defective, stronghold thinking when a characteristic or behavior needs transformation. So, it's unsurprising that God's answer to pride is true humility. Humility loves God's ways more than my ways. Humility trusts Jesus to be my role model and the Holy Spirit to be the source of my attitude. Humility loves others. Humility also loves self in a godly way. We cannot genuinely love others if we don't love ourselves in a healthy and humble way. Humility helps us unlearn the prideful protection mechanisms that built up walls and made our former life comfortable. Putting those coping mechanisms under our feet requires a lot of letting go.

For everyone who exalts himself will be humbled, and the one who humbles himself will be exalted.
Luke 14:11

Heavenly Father, help us recognize when we act out of a prideful heart. Help us see any area of our heart that needs to yield itself to your transformation. Humble us as we trust you to champion the road to freedom. *~Amen.*

Chapter 16

All In

Next to him, Uzziel the son of Harhaiah of the goldsmiths, made repairs. And next to him Hananiah, one of the perfumers, made repairs, and they restored Jerusalem as far as the Broad Wall... Next to him Shallum the son of Hallohesh, the official of half the district of Jerusalem, made repairs, he and his daughters.
Nehemiah 3:8, 12

There weren't many slackers. Most people were all in, and even whole families helped in this manual labor. The task of rebuilding entailed moving huge stones from a pile of rubble and lifting them onto a tall wall. The workers had to spread dirt and gravel around to level places to set the heavy rocks. It was backbreaking, sweaty work that no one enjoyed, yet the people put their regular jobs and daily tasks on hold to do what was needed. That indicates how they were united in pursuing a greater purpose than their own comfort. They were laboring to restore, renew, and invigorate the city of Jerusalem. Rebuilding the wall would bring a season of fresh renewal for everyone.

Today, we see this unity when we have natural disasters like hurricanes, wildfires, and tornadoes. People are passionate about the projects and volunteer to help those affected get through these tragic disasters. We want to help others through a storm. Some people are willing to prepare the level rows and set the heavy rocks, even when it's not what they want to do. We do what is needed because we know that, eventually, it will benefit everyone to renew a community.

I received salvation as a teenager but never quite grasped its meaning. I didn't have the home life to support a Christian journey, so my initial enthusiasm for Jesus faded until I was twenty-nine. I started dating my future husband, and we began attending church regularly. That was the beginning of my real walk as a Christian. At the same time, I started reading the Bible and learning about God. The process was slow because I held onto a lot of sin, yet I ended up with a huge desire to know more about Jesus and to be more like him. My passion to be more like Jesus has continued on a long but progressive journey.

When we are born again, our spirit instantly becomes alive and is transformed into the complete image of God, but our soul (mind, will, emotions) still has its old baggage and ingrained ways of thinking. Our soul is transformed by an ongoing process of willfully renewing our minds with the Word of God. Even though we now have God alive in us, we still need to peel away the layers of our old self (our sinful nature) to reveal more of our new godly nature. The Holy Spirit is a gentleman and doesn't force us to change anything. We choose the timing as we take each step. We start as immature Christians, but he put his complete and whole Spirit into us. The more we learn about God and make choices to surrender the layers of our worldly motivations, the more we grow and mature. We renew our souls by allowing the Holy Spirit to be in control. That's what we do if we are all in.

In the beginning, even though I was growing as a Christian, I didn't want to surrender many things to God. I hung onto sin and various areas of my life: pride, career, food, alcohol, sex, health, and relationships. Withholding these areas from God prevented me from renewing my mind in critical ways. The infrastructure of these mindsets ultimately fell into ruins. I clung to being the god of my life instead of letting Jesus be my Lord in those areas. In fact, I didn't *want* to renew my mind in those parts of my life. I liked being in charge. I wanted to choose the areas I would turn over to God and gradually be transformed in my mind. I didn't want to become one of those Jesus Freaks, so I always held back. I was giving territory to God a little at a time, so I convinced myself I was all in.

To fully renew our minds, we must embrace the way God thinks, and the best place to find out how he thinks is in the Bible. Everything we need to know is available in the Bible, but we need to pull out the book, read it, meditate on it, learn it, agree with it, use it, love it, practice it, and live it. When we seek God, he rewards us with a greater understanding of who he is and his will. We renew our minds by replacing the world's messages with the truth of what God says. But he never forces that growth on us; we must choose it and do it.

And do not be conformed to this world, but be transformed by the renewing of your mind, so that you may prove what the will of God is, that which is good and acceptable and perfect.
Romans 12:2

Father God, your ways are different from how the world wants us to live. The Holy Spirit is nudging us to abandon our old ways. Help us yield our prideful hearts to you so we can be transformed into kingdom-driven, joy-filled Jesus followers. *~Amen.*

Chapter 17

Community

Above the Horse Gate the priests carried out repairs, each in front of his house. After them Zadok the son of Immer carried out repairs in front of his house. And after him Shemaiah the son of Shecaniah, the keeper of the East Gate, carried out repairs.
Nehemiah 3:28–29

Nehemiah strengthened the community by assigning people to work on sections of the wall near their homes. Neighbors worked side by side right in front of their properties. Day after day, the people's bonds were strengthened as they carried out the hard labor together.

I can imagine the scene of a typical day's work rebuilding the walls: kids haul buckets of smaller stones and gravel from here to there. Moms make food, tend gardens and animals, and keep the family businesses afloat. Strong young men use hoists and ropes to lift huge rocks into place. Everyone is sweaty and dusty, but they are in it together.

In a community project like this, people look past their differences with others—the stupid things they said last month, their cheering for the wrong sports team, the way they raise their kids, or the wrong candidate they voted for. The focus must be on the common ground, not the differences. This unity paves the way for our collective success.

In the community, we work alongside our neighbors and learn how to blend each section of the work with the next so that, when we're done, the transition from my piece to yours is unnoticeable to the outside world. Overcoming differences builds continuity in the community.

When I started my healing journey, I was alone. I had no community after being isolated for several years. I had moved a thousand miles away from my friends and family. I didn't have a traditional local church, and my job situation did not work out. The loneliness was overwhelming, but I knew the enemy tried to isolate his prey.

Rebuilding would be rough and even heartbreaking, so I needed encouragement and some community that understood where I was coming from. Otherwise, I would never fit in. I knew I would be moving multiple times, and my transitions would be financially and emotionally challenging—further pointing to my need for connection and support. The kind of support I needed meant three specific things: rekindling friendships, attending church, and participating in small groups.

Rekindling Friendships

When I abruptly remarried and moved away, I left solid friendships in the rearview mirror. A key reason was my guilt and shame, which kept me from being open and honest about my life. Most of those people advised me not to get remarried. When I realized they were right, it was easier to hide. But the Lord prompted me to reestablish a few essential friendships in my new rebuilding season. One friend had moved a few hours away to the same state I was in. She was the first step in being honest with my old friends. These relationships helped me feel loved in my regrets and normal in my awkwardness.

Attending Church

For almost three years, I was involved with a church physically located in Israel. We participated over the internet and with various messaging apps. I began to see problems with the church, its leadership, and its teachings; these escalated to the point where I finally realized that it was a cult. When I came to terms with that, I quickly exited. I was left with a vast amount of church hurt, but that wasn't an excuse to abandon churches altogether. Nope.

After being in a cult, it has taken time and healing to be comfortable calling another church "home." Bad teaching has a way of changing your perspective, so I had to purposefully assess what I am comfortable with in the charismatic community. I had to process through the experiences to find the truth and weigh it against the Word of God.

I needed a place to be with others and worship God. I needed to be in a community of believers. It was hard to do this alone, to show up at a church for the first time and sit in a row of people I'd never seen before. We said an awkward "hello" but then worshiped as a community—a bunch of people together, singing to God. After several years in a long-distance church, worshiping in person with others often brought me to tears. In those tears, I learned to treasure worship in a new way. When I finally had a friend to sit with in church, I actually cried.

Participating in Small Groups

The Christian recovery program I had previously been a part of believed in the forever-family principle, so I began to attend meetings again. Even when I moved to other cities, as part of this organization, I would always have a community of people to plug into. This recovery community consists of people just like me working out their problems, and we all believe Jesus is the solution.

I also found book study groups to participate in. Many churches offer excellent study groups and programs to strengthen and disciple people in their Christian journey. Involvement with study groups helped me understand how to apply Christian principles to my life and build more friendships. During COVID, many great virtual Christian communities popped up that have also been a steady stream of new friendships.

And let's consider how to encourage one another in love
and good deeds, not abandoning our own meeting together, as is the
habit of some people, but encouraging one another; and all the more as
you see the day drawing near.
Hebrews 10:24–25

Lord Jesus, we need each other. Your Word reminds us to get together and encourage each other, so I pray for every reader to search their hearts for ways to stay in community with other believers. Please surround us with those who will help us stay on track. *~Amen.*

Chapter 18

Anger, Offense and Forgiveness

When Sanballat heard that we were rebuilding the wall, he became angry
and was greatly incensed. He ridiculed the Jews, and in the presence of
his associates and the army of Samaria, he said,
"What are those feeble Jews doing?
Nehemiah 4:1–2 NIV

If someone is against you from the start, they can bring trouble
and more trouble. In this story, Nehemiah's adversaries tried to
stir up sentiment against the rebuilding project. If Sanballat and
associates got their way, a whole army would crush the efforts of
the Jews to rebuild the wall.

Sanballat's tactics were not limited to confrontation. He understood the power of influencing public opinion, even without social
media. His approach was similar to today's mainstream media,
which takes a biased stance on a political issue and spreads it
across all news outlets. The aim was to foster a culture of negativity, pessimism, and anger, effectively turning public sentiment
against the Jews and Nehemiah.

Anger can be a symptom of the underlying need to be in control.
Road rage is a fitting example of how someone wants to control
the way others drive. When someone drives poorly, anger can
progress quickly from annoyance to rage over unintentional in-
fractions. In such scenarios, the person blames the other driver
for their aggravation, prompting a perceived need to retaliate to
get justice or revenge.

Sanballat was probably a road rage guy. Nehemiah wasn't.

I never thought of myself as angry, yet I can now see some interesting patterns that reveal anger in disguise. My anger comes out as complaining, fault-finding, blaming, or defensiveness. These behaviors are just as unhealthy as anger manifesting as rage; they just look different and less extreme.

In an argument, my personality type tends to explain my point repeatedly, presuming that if I keep talking, the other person will eventually see the light. If not, I get louder and more emphatic about my point because that will surely help the other person understand better. Sometimes, I recognize when I'm doing this and see that I am stubborn and masking my anger.

Ephesians 4:27 says that if we don't deal with anger immediately, we give the devil an "opportunity" or, as some translations say, a "foothold." Anger doesn't start as a sin but escalates into sin. We need to resolve our differences and forgive others right away, or we give our real enemy, Satan, an open invitation to build a stronghold of resentment, bitterness, and unforgiveness in our souls. Strongholds are ingrained patterns of thinking that become difficult to change.

When genuinely wronged, we may incorrectly assume anger is "righteous" anger. However, righteous anger is when we are mad at *sin*, while carnal anger is directed at the *person*.

Anger's partner is an offense—anger blossoms into offense, which is literally a trap. The original Greek word for *offense*[1] in the Bible also means "a snare" or "a trap." Satan wants to ambush us into offense because he loves to destroy relationships. Especially when the offense seems justified, we harden our hearts with resentments that can last forever.

The more unoffendable I become, the more peaceful I am. The key is to recognize when I am offended or angry and work through it with the Holy Spirit. What am I feeling? Why is this issue irritating me? What part of me is affected or offended: ego, timelines, identity, boundaries, physical, finances, personal goals, patience, or beliefs? Am I trying to be in control? Is someone trying to control me? What is triggering me?

How can I become more unoffendable and resolve my anger?

- **Ask the Holy Spirit** to show me what has offended me. Then, dig a little deeper. What happened? What am I angry about? What part of my nature feels hurt? Was my reaction appropriate or wrong?

- **Repent for wrong reactions that I acted out.** Change always starts with me. In every interaction, I'm responsible for my side of the fence. What am I talking about? An example is road rage. This is a sinful reaction to someone driving incorrectly. A more complex example would be turning to drugs after a traumatic event. We need to understand our wrong behaviors. Please note that we don't accept responsibility for the harm done *to* us, but we do acknowledge our sinful reactions.

- **Forgive.** Forgiving can be complicated. It's easier when the other person is honestly concerned. Ideally, forgiveness directly involves that other person but often will not. Sometimes the other person may not care, may not be repentant, or even realize they did anything wrong. In some cases, they may have already passed away. However, we still benefit from releasing bitterness and moving on emotionally. The kind of forgiveness that frees us may not provide justice, or revenge, or change in the other person. Those outcomes are outside this discussion.

  - **Forgiving is a transaction between God and you.** We ask God to forgive and allow him to deal with the situation. Let his forgiveness flow until there is peace.

  - **Telling someone we forgive them is optional**, depending on the relationship, circumstances, and wisdom. Forgiving them doesn't mean *they* are sorry. They may never have remorse or change their actions. In those cases, we may need to work out our hurt privately without saying anything to them.

  - **Reconciliation is optional.** If it is appropriate to mend the relationship by talking to the person, then we should do it, but forgiveness and reconciliation are separate issues. Forgiveness is not trust. Reconciliation may not always be advisable, so don't assume you have to reconcile with toxic or unsafe people as part of forgiveness. We are called to forgive but not necessarily to resume a relationship.

○ **Forgiveness is freeing.** When we accept that we need to forgive, God can step into the situation for us and begin the healing. We can let God's forgiving power wash over the situation and cleanse our souls from bitterness toward that person. God is gentle with us and gives us grace until we are ready to forgive. But the longer we wait to forgive, the stronger the roots of bitterness become.

- **Refill your emptiness.** Ask the Holy Spirit to fill any emptiness that remains.

- **Bless others.** Instead of being bitter, pray for them to be blessed. Once forgiveness is complete, you will even want to bless those who have hurt you deeply.

- If you still feel offended, forgiveness may be incomplete.

In my walk toward freedom, nothing has healed me more than forgiving. It released the pain in my soul, even if I never told the offenders about my struggle.

Don't forget to forgive yourself. Your choices, reactions, and preferences are part of the equation. Release yourself from the weight of your mistakes.

What about "forgiving" God? For the record, God never did anything wrong, but we often blame him when we don't like what happened. If you think God didn't do what he was supposed to, e.g., protect you, answer your prayer, save your family members, you may need to work through a process of releasing him from your idea of how it should have turned out.

In Mark 12:30–31, Jesus summarized all the commandments of the law into just two: love God and love people. Learning to love others the way Jesus did gives me clues about overcoming anger and offense. Whenever I choose to love other people instead of hanging onto offense, I lay another brick in my road to freedom.

In your anger do not sin: Do not let the sun go down while you are still angry, and do not give the devil a foothold... Be kind and compassionate to one another, forgiving each other, just as in Christ God forgave you.
Ephesians 4:26–27, 32 NIV

Heavenly Father, anger and offense so easily trap us. Help every reader recognize when an offense is taking a foothold and how it wants to destroy our relationships. Through your loving-kindness, we learn to be forgiving and compassionate, so I pray we embrace your way of dealing with anger. It is counterintuitive but brings freedom to our souls. Thank you for freeing us from the weight of offense. *~In Jesus' powerful name, we pray. Amen.*

Chapter 19

Lies

And he spoke in the presence of his brothers and the wealthy people of Samaria and said, "What are these feeble Jews doing? Are they going to restore the temple for themselves? Can they offer sacrifices? Can they finish it in a day? Can they revive the stones from the heaps of rubble, even the burned ones?" Now Tobiah the Ammonite was near him, and he said, "Even what they are building—if a fox were to jump on it, it would break their stone wall down!"
Nehemiah 4:2–3

Nehemiah and the people of Jerusalem had to put up with ongoing harassment and intimidation while they rebuilt their walls. The enemies used bad-mouthing, name-calling, gossip, propaganda, and outright slander to turn people against each other. Lies spread like an infection, ruining morale and discouraging the workers.

Consider this: even falsehoods can appear plausible when mudslinging originates from a credible source. But when a stealthy adversary orchestrates it, disparaging words can transform a small pocket of disagreement into a tidal wave of opposition. This is because mudslinging and bullying are often team efforts. Once the leader initiates a campaign of lies, others join in, reinforcing and encouraging each other with more falsehoods.

These bad guys were trying to build an army of opposition to the rebuilding project by convincing people to believe lies. We're all guilty of occasionally participating in these rhetoric wars, particularly during election seasons. We hear lies mixed in with some truth, which makes us think that what we hear is believable. When a measure of truth is involved, we readily believe falsehoods because they sound more probable. These lying mudslingers assumed this worthy project was doomed to fail, but history proved them wrong.

I have been on both sides of this sin: I was a verbal bully as a kid. I was also profoundly harmed by words as an adult.

I did not grow up in a Christian home and learned how to cut other people down from hearing my parents argue. I became one of those popular, mean girls, bullying and belittling others, and saying many unkind things. As a young adult, I admired sarcasm and witty put-downs. Since then, I have learned about the intense damage that results from these behaviors. I completely regret all my unkind behavior now because I know the kind of damage words can cause. I am incredibly sorry for my hurtful words in elementary and middle school. As I grew and matured as a Christian, I outgrew these awful behaviors. Interestingly, however, I ended up being their recipient. We reap what we sow.

Harsh words are verbal lies that hurt us. An example is when someone takes a flaw and accentuates it. The worst lies also fall into the realm of deception and abuse because they take a little bit of truth and a little bit of untruth and blend them to make us feel rejected.

Here are some examples of lies that Satan uses to make us feel inadequate and destroy relationships:

- How can you be so stupid?

- I wish you had never been born.

- You should be ashamed of yourself.

- You make my life miserable.

- You never do anything right.

- My ex was better than you at...

Words *do* matter because our hearts believe what we hear. I have listened to many words that made me feel unloved and worthless because my heart believed what was said. But the worst thing was what I said about myself. It is harder to erase the damage that comes out of our own mouths. Believing those lies spoken to us can generate a hierarchy of new lies in our minds. These become strongholds. Negative words we speak attack our very identity when we say, "I am..."

- I'm so ugly.

- I am all alone.

- I will never be able to make enough money.

- I can't do anything right.

- I will never have a good job.

- I will never be loved.

- I am such a failure.

These kinds of statements are lies from the pit of hell. We have already discussed how to appropriate our identity in Christ with the truth about what God says about us, but we also need to crush the lies. We must stop *believing* and reinforcing them.

My love language[1] is words of affirmation. Life is kind of funny like that. I desperately needed to hear that I was loved unconditionally, but I did not choose men who encouraged me in that way. Thankfully, I have a Father in heaven who keeps telling me:

- I am loved.

- I am loved.

- I am loved.

Do not lie to one another, since you stripped off the old self with its evil practices, and have put on the new self, which is being renewed to a true knowledge according to the image of the One who created it.
Colossians 3:9–10

God, words hurt. Words have hurt every one of us, including me. Please help me stop believing the lies and hear your voice over the enemy's lies. Lord, renew me into your image so I can confidently destroy the old self that was driven by lies and hurtful protection mechanisms. Your ways are better than mine. *~Amen.*

Chapter 20

Blessings and Curses

Hear, O our God, for we are despised; turn their reproach on their own
heads, and give them as plunder to a land of captivity! Do not cover their
iniquity, and do not let their sin be blotted out from before You; for they
have provoked You to anger before the builders.
Nehemiah 4:4–5 NKJV

Nehemiah turned to God to deal with the bullies rather than trying
to correct them or argue with them. Good for him. However, Nehemiah asks for vengeance on his enemies in this prayer because
they were taunting the builders and God himself. God blessed this
project, so enemies of the work were enemies of God. Nehemiah's
response was to ask God to curse these guys. As an Old Testament
story, before the new covenant of grace through Jesus, people
commonly prayed for God's justice this way.

What is a curse, anyway? I looked it up, and according to the
Oxford English Dictionary[1], a *curse* is "a solemn utterance intended to invoke a supernatural power to inflict harm or punishment
on someone or something."

Curses, as we understand them, come in various forms. In the
Bible, however, they are often associated with God's direct intervention, inflicting harm or punishment upon individuals, places,
or even entire nations. In the Old Testament, God, in his wisdom,
outlined the behaviors that would lead to such consequences and
his intended response. So, people in Nehemiah's time asked God
to punish others when faced with injustices and wrong behaviors.

In the New Testament, we learn how to deal with enemies differently. Jesus took on all the punishment at the cross and became the curse we deserved. He even took the curses our enemies deserved! This is talked about in Galatians 3:13, saying: Christ redeemed us from the curse of the Law, having become a curse for us.

Because Jesus took all punishment for all humanity upon himself, we are not to be the source of revenge, nor should we even wish adverse outcomes upon others—yet we do. How often do we feel justified in hoping the evil actions of people will result in as much trouble in their lives as they have given us? Or worse?

Examples of how we commonly speak curses over people include things like telling someone to "go to hell" or "damn you." That usually is a punishment much greater than the thing that occurred. Or what about the saying "Shame on you"? That is a subtle curse, heaping shame and condemnation on someone. Why do we say that?

In my darkest season, when the wrongs and abuses of others were crushing me, I justified hurling curses by the world's standards. But all I could muster up during the worst of my prolonged nightmare was feelings of hate accompanied by crying. I felt like everyone in my life either misunderstood or rejected me—or both. These feelings reinforced my walls of bitterness and resentment. I kept trying different strategies, but none of them improved the situation.

As I exited those negative situations, my mind cleared, and the truth came into focus as I sought help and a solid, biblical direction for overcoming my devastation. A tiny truth made a dramatic difference: I had to forgive and bless them. My first reaction was, "*Whaaat?* Bless them? Really?" That seemed like a big stretch. I had worked on forgiving myself, but now I had to start forgiving others.

I made a list of resentments toward those who had wronged me and presented them to God; then, I worked through it all with him (and often with a prayer minister). Jesus is the forgiver, and I must open the door to forgiveness to let him free my heart from its dungeon of offense. Until I am willing, God will not violate my choices. He honors my decision if I continue with the sins of resentment and unforgiveness. If I choose forgiveness, he gladly releases me from my bitterness.

A sign of true forgiveness is peace and speaking blessings over those who have hurt us. If we can't bless someone, then our forgiveness is probably incomplete. Some offenses are much harder to forgive than others. Some I am still working on. However, I tackled most of the big ones first to find some peace. I continue to pray for the people who have caused me the most significant harm to keep my heart from moving back into resentment. When a memory torments me, I know I must take that to God. God can decide if punishment is needed. My only job is to be at peace enough to speak blessings and pray for those people.

I had to move these heavy boulders in my rebuilding process. Clearing and placing them underfoot led to triumph and victory, forever changing my life.

But I say to you who hear, love your enemies,
do good to those who hate you, bless those who curse you,
pray for those who are abusive to you.
Luke 6:27–28

Jesus, only through you can we learn to bless our enemies. This is hard for us, and you know it. Please give us the desire in our hearts to handle life like you did. We cannot do this alone. *~Amen.*

Chapter 21

The Easy Half

So we rebuilt the wall till all of it reached half its height, for the people
worked with all their heart.
Nehemiah 4:6 NIV

The people of Jerusalem passionately worked on the wall and quickly made considerable progress. The fact that they worked "with all their heart" shows their enthusiasm and unity. That feeling comes more easily during the first sprint in a project when people's energy is focused as they excitedly see actual accomplishments. But when building walls, the higher you go, the harder the job is.

The wall around Jerusalem today is about forty feet high, about the equivalent of a three to four-story building. It's also about eight feet thick, so if an army comes by and pushes most of it down, the part near the ground will stay relatively intact while the higher parts will fall over. When you try to put the wall back together again, most of the first few rows of stone blocks are likely to already be in place. The next few rows may be easy to set in, but by the time you've built a twenty-foot wall, you probably think that's good enough.

Yet good enough is not synonymous with excellence, and a wall that's half the needed height is far from complete. The builders understood they had a long and challenging journey ahead, and what they had accomplished so far was the easy half.

Be thankful for the easy parts and be ready for the challenging parts.

As I previously mentioned, I was restarting my life at fifty-nine years old. I thought leaving a cult and the abusive four-year marriage would be challenging, but that turned out to be the easy part. Starting over in multiple locations was even harder. In two years, I made three long-distance moves, totaling almost 2,500 miles. I did this while getting my career back on track and stabilizing my emotional, financial, and spiritual life. Being older, alone, and moving across the country is not easy. The first half of my life seemed easier than what I was dealing with now.

I ended up in a city where I had lived for a few years as a young adult. It had changed significantly but still seemed somewhat familiar. The most important benefit of moving to this new city was that an old friend was now living there, so I had one safe and loving person to lean on. What a blessing! She invited me to activities and events hosted by her church's Christian singles group. She introduced me to her friends. She kept encouraging me to do what I didn't want to do. I was okay with going alone to check out different churches, but hanging out with normal people had become *waaay* out of my comfort zone. But my friend persisted. Afraid and awkward, I was stepping out and making new friends. Not dating, but going to events like speakers and discussion groups, games, hikes, kayaking, and potlucks. Wholesome activities. It was so hard, but it was good for me.

I set a non-negotiable daily activity: get out of the house. Since I was working from home, it was easy to stay inside. Instead, I forced myself to go for a walk, an errand, or a drive every day.

As with many of the spiritual principles we are looking at, we most often need to do the opposite of what we *want* to do. We need to do hard things when we are afraid and uncomfortable. Our natural self will want to isolate, and that is just what our enemy, Satan, wants for us. If I'm lonely, I need to interact with people. If I am offended, I need to respond with forgiveness. If I feel financially insecure, I need to be generous. Building spiritual muscle is similar to building physical muscles. By stretching and working, we build muscles in areas where we are weak.

Satan wants to isolate us, destroying our relationships and tempting us to build more walls so no one can penetrate our defenses. Living behind walls may be our hiding place, but our freedom comes by walking the road of truth. Our battle is to keep building the road outward, even when it's hard.

Whatever you do, do your work heartily, as for the Lord and not for people, knowing that it is from the Lord that you will receive the reward of the inheritance. It is the Lord Christ whom you serve.
Colossians 3:23–24

Father God, we know that every part of life has its challenges. I just pray for everyone reading to trust that our reward is in heaven, even when we don't see it here on earth. That's not easy, but the reward is great when we do it for you. ~*Amen.*

Chapter 22

Confusion

> Now when Sanballat, Tobiah, the Arabs, the Ammonites, and the Ashdodites heard that the repair of the walls of Jerusalem went on, and that the breaches began to be closed, they were very angry. So all of them conspired together to come to fight against Jerusalem and to cause confusion in it.
> Nehemiah 4:7–8

Sometimes, troublemakers won't go away. Sometimes, they gain strength by recruiting others. They plot and lurk in the shadows, figuring out how to ambush us. They try to build fear, disrupt life, and convince you to take your focus off the goals. A key revelation in these verses is that the enemies were trying to cause confusion. Some Bible translations say they were "stirring up trouble." Confusion and trouble against an effort like building the wall would focus on destroying the enthusiasm of the builders and undermining Nehemiah's leadership. Enemies like to confuse their rivals. Confused people don't form effective teams. Creating confusion about a project causes arguments, criticism, and, most of all, complaints.

Sometimes, the enemy is short-sighted. In this case, harassment made the builders even more determined to complete their goal. For the people in Jerusalem, the threat of attack was an incentive to work with more passion and determination as it became increasingly clear that a thick, high wall was more important than ever. The threats accentuated their need for protection because walls meant peace and safety for them.

I experienced so much emotional confusion as I began to leave my brokenness behind. Some of the difficulties I had to overcome were the effects of brainwashing, manipulation, and the twisting of Scripture by those closest to me. These traumas created a kind of brain fog that affected my ability to focus on my job, make decisions, plan activities, and just live. My emotional state has improved steadily throughout the years of rebuilding, but it continues to be a problem sometimes. Because of occasional fogginess, I still have trouble deciding what to do in a few areas. Sometimes, I realize an entire day has blown by, and I accomplished nothing.

An ironic example of this confusion is how it has taken me a month to write this particular chapter. I drafted other chapters in a few hours or days, but I could not figure out what to say about this topic of confusion. I would have a spurt of inspiration that made me feel like I was successfully fighting off the problem. I'd write a few paragraphs, but when I reviewed them, they did not even come close to conveying the point I thought I was making. Other times, the progress seemed negligible, and I started over again. When this happens, I've found it is a clue that I am under spiritual attack. If the target keeps shifting, it's likely I am experiencing spiritual issues. No peace comes in my work when dealing with a spiritual problem.

I have also found that distraction and confusion are good buddies. We have all distracted ourselves by scrolling through social media, sometimes called doomscrolling. We scroll and scroll. And scroll. And scroll. Those sneaky little demons want to keep us from being productive. When I feel confused, unsettled, foggy, or distracted, I struggle to stop and redirect my thinking, which is precisely what I need to do. Even the secular world has recognized the need to be mindful of our thinking and shift gears when needed. Our hearts are looking for peace, but it can be challenging to identify when we are overwhelmed and need to make that shift.

The apostle Paul had to help the church in Corinth navigate the cultural disruptions confusing their church services. He was helping them overcome their former pagan traditions when he said:

"For God is not a God of confusion, but of peace" (1 Corinthians 14:33).

In our confusion, we can find peace by learning to abide extra in the Holy Spirit, inviting him to walk with us in all we do. We can make that necessary shift into peace as soon as we realize we are in confusion or distraction mode. Refocus on peace and pray for more of it. Do it when you don't feel like it. Ask the Holy Spirit to continue filling you daily so you can have more peace.

More peace means more clarity and the ability to focus on the right things.

Peace I leave you, My peace I give you; not as the world gives, do I give to you. Do not let your hearts be troubled, nor fearful.
John 14:27

Lord Jesus, I pray for all the readers to seek your peace—the way out of confusion and anxiety. You are the peace our hearts need. As we abide in you, our peace comes. *~Amen.*

Chapter 23

On Guard

But we prayed to our God, and because of them we set up a guard against them day and night.
Nehemiah 4:9

First, Nehemiah sought God's wisdom before he acted with his own wisdom. When we go to God first, we can ask him what *he* has to say about our situation. He can inform us of the dangers ahead and help us see what action will keep us safe.

While trusting God to bless the project, Nehemiah took practical steps by posting physical guards to protect the city. God did not place a mystical, supernatural bubble over Jerusalem to protect it from the realities of the world around it. God occasionally will supernaturally eliminate an enemy, but in this case, he didn't stop the attacks against the construction project. The people still needed to deter their worldly enemies with earthly physical weapons. Specifically, that meant men with swords patrolled the city's perimeter all day and night.

To guard something is to keep it safe from harm and be willing to defend it if necessary. The project's goal was to provide the citizens with a safer city, so it made sense to do everything possible to keep them safe while doing the work. That protection included swords, arrows, and guards.

Modern protection mechanisms do not include swords. Some of us live in unsafe neighborhoods that may require extra caution and sometimes weapons, especially after dark. But more often, modern guard duty is emotional. It may include turning off social media; avoiding or blocking toxic people, places, and websites; dropping certain activities; or managing health and finances more effectively. If we have full-blown addictions, then guarding ourselves has failed somewhere along the way, and focused recovery is needed.

In personal relationships, guarding ourselves is a whole different ball game. I don't know how you grew up, but my family was quite dysfunctional. The family dynamics taught me how to protect myself from those closest to me by keeping my heart cold and hardened so that I wouldn't be hurt when they eventually abandoned or rejected me. I watched my parents tear each other down with words and then act like nothing happened. There was no forgiving that I can remember—just cold coexistence until the next blowup. I saw my parents' marriage crumble, and when it finally fell apart, I was glad because the fighting stopped.

Even as a young girl, I started learning how to build walls. I let my heart harden like bricks so I could have solid walls to protect me from the inevitable rejection. The funny thing is that a heart as hard as bricks is often a heart full of fear masked with a shiny layer of pride, so others won't see the vulnerabilities. In a relationship, I needed affirmation that I was loved, but that's not what I got. I was in constant fear of being abandoned because of continued verbal rejection. My walls comforted me and seemed to protect my heart from breaking. Of course, that didn't work.

Eventually, my heart was smashed to smithereens, and God placed me on a path of healing. I began to learn about and use a healthy alternative to building walls in relationships—it's called boundaries. Boundaries can be healthy (or unhealthy) ways to limit how we interact with others. I learned (too late) that I don't have to participate in repetitive arguments and that I could say no to harmful behavior. I learned the impact it was having on me and my impact on others. It took a long time to say no because

I always hoped someone else would change. Unfortunately, we can only change ourselves. Adding some boundaries to relational dynamics can be tricky, but we *can* begin to connect with others differently. Instead of trying to hide our innermost unmet needs, we can communicate truthfully with ourselves and others about how we are feeling. We can change our reactions and relationship with God, but we cannot expect to change others around us.

Guarding our hearts is done through the peace of God, not by our reactions, manipulation, pleading, hiding, numbing, cowering, acting tough, retaliating, scheming, or finding comfort in the world. It is by finding comfort in God. Abiding in him is our peace. We can open our hearts to the truth and peace of God instead of trying to manage the fear with false protection mechanisms.

As in the previous chapter, we learn that God has peace for us in difficult situations. It doesn't make sense, but it is true. When I stopped reacting from a position of fear, I found peace. And when I guard my heart with peace instead of fear, the enemy can do nothing to hurt me.

And the peace of God, which surpasses all comprehension, will guard your hearts and minds in Christ Jesus.
Philippians 4:7

God, so many have no peace in their lives and are trying to discover what this even means. You are the only true source of peace that can guard us, so I pray for that peace to be generously poured out on the hearts and minds of every reader. *~In the powerful name of Jesus, I pray. ~Amen.*

And Lord, I pray an extra prayer for anyone in an actively abusive relationship. Help them see a road to safety and give them hope in both the natural and the spiritual areas of their lives. Finding peace may seem far away, so please provide a glimpse of what that looks like and give them special blessings as they find a way to guard their hearts. *~Amen.*

Chapter 24

Discouraged

Meanwhile, the people in Judah said, "The strength of the laborers is
giving out, and there is so much rubble
that we cannot rebuild the wall."
Nehemiah 4:10 NIV

When all you see is rubble everywhere, it's hard to imagine a
future without it—you can't see a way out of the wreckage even
when you're working to overcome it. After laboring day after
day, the builders were becoming exhausted, overwhelmed, and
burned out. They had accomplished so much but had a long
way to go. The people working with Nehemiah were becoming
discouraged.

The builders were now working on the part of the wall more
than twenty feet above ground. They needed to move blocks
that were too heavy and too large into places that were way too
high. It is not easy to take blocks from the piles of rubble and
then maneuver them thirty or forty feet high. Wow! Building
walls was exhausting work.

Through the lens of the rubble, this kind of repair project
seemed overwhelming and even defeating. Discouragement
came to the builders in the second half of the project as the
work became more challenging and the opposition increased.
Defeat started to seem more likely. The workers were from a
generation that had never even seen the wall in its prior glory.
From their perspective, the wall had always been a scene of
wreckage and rebuilding it looked more impossible by the day.
And they knew that the most challenging part of the project
was yet to come.

Overcoming discouragement is difficult when you are still deep in the circumstances causing the problems. There may seem to be no hope, and life beyond the wreckage is nowhere in sight, especially when you have never even seen success. Like the builders, we could live life from one disaster to the next, never able to see past the rubble.

At my breaking point, I could not see how to get free. My perspective was from the rubble, which was piling higher and higher. I had no hope and was discouraged. Then, God created a small opening and then another and another. I wasn't emotionally ready for any of these steps, so I just took them in desperation and trusted God's plan even though I couldn't see it. As I took each step in faith, I moved another brick from my pile of rubble. And then another.

One day, I started to see the light ahead on my path toward freedom. Finally, I had some hope as I saw just a peek of God's glory out there in the distance. Each step was like moving a huge boulder. Though it was hard, as I finished each step, I knew I could take another. When living through the lens of disaster, all I could see was one defeat after another, but eventually, I could see one victory after another. I then started to see life from the perspective of an overcomer: from one victory to the next.

In the middle of the mess, someone shared a verse about living from glory to glory, but I couldn't understand what it meant because I was in a pit of deep discouragement. It was like confusion fogged up my comprehension. Interestingly enough, that is precisely what the verse is talking about. It uses the metaphor of a veil over our faces. When unveiled, we see the glory of the Lord within us. When consumed with our old thinking patterns, we will be stuck in the rubble and only measure life from one defeat to the next. We must remove the veil to transform our perspective and see the truth. This transformation means searching out our blind spots, moving out of denial, assessing the damage, and saying no to what is harming us.

When we choose to live from the perspective of the Holy Spirit, he unveils the truth to us and guides, comforts, and empowers us.

We are living a life upgraded by God. In this upgraded life, we can measure our successes, not our defeats.

I have transformed my perspective so I can see glory and victory. Hallelujah!

But we all, with unveiled faces, looking as in a mirror at the glory of the Lord, are being transformed into the same image from glory to glory, just as from the Lord, the Spirit.
2 Corinthians 3:18

Lord, you can transform us so we can live from glory to glory instead of defeat to defeat. Unveil our hearts so your freedom can transform us. Unveil our understanding to see you in the valleys and the mountaintops. Thank you, Holy Spirit, for leading us into the next victory of glory. *~Amen.*

Chapter 25

Death Threats

And our enemies said, "They will not know or see until we come among
them, kill them, and put a stop to the work."
Nehemiah 4:11

Since the Garden of Eden, enemies have tried to sneak in and kill
every good thing we are doing. In the garden, there was a successful attack to keep Adam and Eve away from the Tree of Life.
Adam and Eve enjoyed an ideal life and had a perfect relationship
with God, yet they chose the way of the world by eating from the
Tree of the Knowledge of Good and Evil. Adam and Eve let their
desire for knowledge take over, and their disobedience produced
the ultimate outcome of sin: death. Their descendants have been
choosing the way of death ever since.

Nehemiah's enemies stepped up their intimidation to an ultimate level: death threats. In their attempt to stop the Jews from
rebuilding the walls of their city, they continued to use fear tactics
to shut down everything. We can deal with killers like these in a
few ways:

1. **Surrender**: We can give in and let the enemy choke our
   productivity and live under control and torment.

2. **Avoid, run, and hide**: Sometimes, we can avoid an attack
   by staying out of sight and evading the enemy. In a project like rebuilding the walls, avoiding it would probably
   involve stopping work until the tension and the political
   climate changed.

3. **Diplomacy**: We can try negotiating, but Nehemiah had

already tried diplomacy, and his enemies countered with more significant threats.

4. **Put on armor:** We can protect ourselves and continue to advance. We must be realistic about the risks, persevere through the harassment, and still work with an attitude of excellence.

Jesus talked about death in a surprising and countercultural way that pointed to something good. He said we would have to die so we could become something more.

"Truly, truly I say to you, unless a grain of wheat falls into the earth and dies, it remains alone; but if it dies, it bears much fruit." (John 12:24).

The apostles taught in greater depth about the way of death that produces new life. However, this insight only came after Jesus' resurrection and the outpouring of the Holy Spirit. With the help of the Holy Spirit, we can see how trapped we are in our sinful ways. Once we make Jesus our Lord and are born again, we begin to see sin for what it is. We can let our old life die and begin to grow and blossom in God's ways instead of the world's ways.

The notion of crucifying our carnal behaviors only makes sense after we see how Jesus gave up everything to go to the cross. It took great love and sacrifice for Jesus to choose that path. When we understand the depth of Jesus' choice, we can follow his model for killing everything in us that still lives for fleshly gratification.

But it isn't just the cross that gives us the power to crucify our sinful ways. The cross motivates us, but the power to change comes through resurrection. We nail our sins on the cross, but the Holy Spirit helps us do it. The Holy Spirit is full of resurrection power and gives us the strength to *keep* our sins nailed to the cross rather than returning and taking them back home.

Still, we continue to struggle with sin. The desires of our flesh are strong. Checking out Facebook is easier than writing a book. Eating cake sometimes seems more comforting than praying. Maybe a little white lie is okay if it keeps the peace. Perhaps it's only human to have an outburst of anger or belittling or gossiping, even after we promised never to do it again. Or buy something when we don't have the money. Or engage in a behavior that we know is wrong but haven't entirely admitted to ourselves it is an addiction or even struggle with a full-blown addiction that we can't stop. And what about that secret sin we just can't quite let go of and hope no one will find out? These are the realities of our sinful nature. And God says we must kill—crucify, actually—these things.

If we keep living the way we have always lived, we will not embrace the intended life of a Christian. The freedom Christ has for us occurs when we let our old selves die. Like seeds, our old ways must be buried to achieve their fruit-bearing potential. They die when we bury them at the cross.

For we know that our old self was crucified with him so that the body ruled by sin might be done away with, that we should no longer be slaves to sin because anyone who has died has been set free from sin.
Romans 6:6–7 NIV

Lord Jesus, it's hard to let go of the behaviors and beliefs that comforted us in the past, but this is the new life you promised. You gave us the Holy Spirit to empower us to do it, but we must take action to crucify what we don't need. Help us want a new life more than we want to continue in the comfortable ways of our past. ~*Amen.*

Chapter 26

Fear

Then the Jews who lived near them came and told us ten times over,
"Wherever you turn, they will attack us."
Nehemiah 4:12 NIV

What's worse than a neighbor who stops by ten times to talk about the worst-case scenario? Some people thrive on discussing all the potential catastrophes. They love listening to the news and speculating about all the fearful events on the horizon. Complainers and negative thinkers increase anxiety but think they mean well.

Now, in addition to the external enemies hurling threats at the builders, a new enemy—fear—was moving through the community. Nehemiah was the kind of person who would show them how to put their faith in the power of God. God would protect the work they were commissioned to do. Threats and risks would come and go, but Nehemiah would not let fear win. He wasn't going to let it take over because wise leaders know the deadly fruit of fear:

- Fear feeds doubt.

- Fear is exhausting.

- Fear steals focus.

- Fear drains motivation.

- And worst of all, fear lives right next door to defeat.

The biggest ongoing fear in rebuilding my life has been my finances. At my age, I qualified for senior discounts, but I had no money left in my retirement account. I had a massive pile of debt along with both career and confidence issues. On a couple of occasions, fear completely overwhelmed me because so much of my life was imploding. But through each crisis, I learned new lessons about standing in faith and not listening to the negative self-talk. I started trusting God to take care of me during these storms.

A monumental breakthrough in this area came shortly after I left the safety of my brother's house and moved to a new state. My remote job abruptly ended only one week after I moved into my new apartment. I had just spent all my savings on the thousand-mile move, but suddenly and unexpectedly, I faced a job search in an area where I had no connections. In my field of work, it usually takes several months to get hired, yet to pay my rent, I needed a job within a few weeks—a complete impossibility. I was overcome with fear, but I approached the situation with a level of faith and surrender I didn't even realize was in me.

I had an unrealistic time frame, and I needed a miracle.

I had faced several financial crises before but approached this one differently. I was now willing to file for bankruptcy and sell my remaining possessions if I needed to. I symbolically laid everything I had at the cross in complete surrender. I had to completely trust God for the solution, knowing that whatever the outcome, I would somehow eventually be okay, even if it meant disaster in the short run.

Meanwhile, my best friend in Phoenix saw how stressed I was, so she bought me a ticket to visit for a week of refreshing and renewal. I couldn't possibly go. I had to continue applying for jobs, be available for interviews, and stay in charge of my situation. I had to fix this. But I couldn't. I did my part and even had a couple of great interviews. Now, I needed to trust God to handle his part (the miracle part!).

I could do nothing more to have the money by the end of the month, and I honestly needed a refreshing break, so I agreed to go. Going on that trip was one of the biggest acts of faith I have ever made.

The time limit for my required miracle was expiring, and that timeline became even more unrealistic. I needed a job offer when I stepped onto the plane for my trip, or I had no hope of paying bills at month end. I accepted the possibility of exploring bankruptcy on my return, assuming that was the likely outcome. I had to let God solve this problem because all my options were exhausted.

But God had something up his sleeve. I was at the airport, waiting to board the plane, when I checked my email. There was the exact job offer I needed. Yes, this is a true story! I could start that job the day after I returned from my visit and have a paycheck to cover my rent at the end of the month. Fighting fear with faith sometimes has fantastic outcomes.

On an interesting side note, my new job was working for a Christian man who named his company after Nehemiah. For a special project, I was able to write a fifty-two-day devotional highlighting the leadership of Nehemiah. That devotional became the outline for this book.

And the Lord said to Paul by a vision at night, "Do not be afraid any longer, but go on speaking and do not be silent; for I am with you, and no one will attack you to harm you, for I have many people in this city."
Acts 18:9–10

God, you have repeatedly proven you can blast through our fears with unexpected blessings and provision. When fear controls us, it wins. When we relax from fear enough to embrace your way of life, your plan for us can unfold, and your blessing can prevail. Thank you for showing us a different way. *~Amen.*

Chapter 27

Vulnerable Places

Therefore I stationed some of the people behind the lowest points of the wall at the exposed places, posting them by families, with their swords, spears and bows.
Nehemiah 4:13 NIV

It's crucial to assign capable individuals to appropriate roles. Nehemiah assessed the placement of guards and provided them with suitable equipment for safeguarding their areas because any gaps could allow the enemies to sneak in. Nehemiah wisely placed the best available resources in the most vulnerable places.

When adversaries are on the horizon, it's crucial to be prepared. The optimal response is to be stationed, well-armed, and self-assured. Therefore, it is essential to establish a defensive position, ensure your weapons are handy, and stay ready.

Nehemiah strategically positioned people to intimidate the enemy forces when they arrived. He wanted their first glimpse of Jerusalem to be of armed guards stationed all around the city, especially where the wall was most likely to be breached, in the most vulnerable places. The builders were not a professionally trained army, but they were the next best thing: men ready to protect their loved ones.

The Holy Spirit is a gentleman who will reveal what to work on at the right time. In recovery, it's called peeling our onion because we all have so many issues that it's impossible to address everything at once. So, we focus on the next issue causing us difficulty—the most vulnerable places that expose us to enemy attacks.

Examining our vulnerable places, we concentrate on whatever the Holy Spirit highlights. We can tell what vulnerable areas need work by looking at behaviors that cause us imbalance or disruption. Here are examples of some common vulnerabilities people struggle with today:

- Addictive tendencies: food, drugs, alcohol, porn, sex and love addiction, gambling, smoking, shopping, excessive fitness, self-image, gaming, social media, codependency, etc.

- Behavioral issues: anger, bullying, arrogance, greed, pride, defensiveness, self-hatred, and a victim mentality.

- Integrity issues: lying, affairs, stealing, gossip, manipulation and control, intimidation, hypocrisy, being on time, and keeping promises.

- False beliefs related to God: idols, cults, occult, astrology, psychics, yoga, new age, Eastern religions, and animism.

- Unforgiveness (a considerable area of vulnerability), which leaves us wide open to bitterness and resentment.

- Unbelief: failure to trust God's promises or will for us.

- Special vulnerabilities that require unique care: mental health, betrayal, harassment, trauma, and any kind of abuse.

- There are many more vulnerable areas of unmet needs, unhealed hurts, and unresolved issues that need attention in our rebuilding process over time.

When addressing many of these areas, we often start in a denial phase where we don't recognize the magnitude of the issues. We may compare ourselves to others, thinking, *I'm not as bad as so-and-so*, but we may have already progressed beyond our ability to eliminate the problem on our own.

We need to tackle these vulnerabilities in our character to avoid additional enemy attacks. We guard ourselves by working on our issues, not by ignoring them, so when the Holy Spirit nudges us, we have the choice to deal with a problem or not. He doesn't rush, force, or give us too much to do. *But*...not working on what God points out may expose us to undesirable consequences. God doesn't spare us from the negative results of our poor choices.

James 4:17 reminds us, "Remember, it is sin to know what you ought to do and then not do it" (NIV).

What does it look like to work on it? Every issue is different, but the healing process usually includes these or similar steps:

- **Acknowledge**: The churchy word for this is to ***confess***. First, we must honestly acknowledge that we must change and accept responsibility for our actions. Once we admit that we need to change, we can trust that God will help us. God is the source of our healing and freedom. While confessing your sins to someone else benefits your healing, confessing does not require a special priest. If you don't have a safe confidant, talk to Jesus directly.

- **Repent**: This means to change our mind about the situation and come into agreement with God about the behavior, with no more debate. You ask God to forgive you for the wrong and commit to changing. It may be beneficial to note that if we are already Christians, we do not repent to make us more holy or to solidify our promise of heaven. Salvation has already accomplished these things. We now repent to heal our souls.

  - According to John Loren Sandford[1]: "Repentance means coming to sufficient hatred of our sins... because we really do not want them any longer."

- **Renounce**: Formally resign from the sinful behavior!

- **Refill**: Ask the Holy Spirit to fill every vulnerable place.

- **Commit**: Here, we implement actions to stop the behavior by asking the Holy Spirit how to change permanently. We decide how to live differently in the future and plan how to incorporate the changes.

It may help to have an accountability partner.

- **Live:** Do the change.

  ○ Continue doing the change even when it feels uncomfortable.

  ○ Continue doing the change even when you don't feel like it.

  ○ Continue doing the change even when tempted to go back.

  ○ Continue doing the change. Period.

Remember that changing is how we fight the enemy and close our gaping holes of vulnerability. It's hard, but it moves boulders.

Looking at the man, Jesus felt genuine love for him. "There is still one thing you haven't done," he told him. "Go and sell all your possessions and give the money to the poor, and you will have treasure in heaven. Then come, follow me." At this the man's face fell, and he went away sad, for he had many possessions. Jesus looked around and said to his disciples, "How hard it is for the rich to enter the Kingdom of God!"
Mark 10:21–23 NLT

Oh, God, many of our vulnerable places still hurt and represent wounds we would rather forget about. Thank you for walking us through the changes we need and for loving us through our challenges and our messes. *~Amen.*

Chapter 28

Focused

When I saw their fear, I stood and said to the nobles, the officials, and the rest of the people: "Do not be afraid of them; remember the Lord who is great and awesome, and fight for your brothers, your sons, your daughters, your wives, and your houses."
Nehemiah 4:14

Nehemiah showed outstanding leadership as he addressed the situation and refocused the people. They were afraid and needed encouragement. Nehemiah first reminds these citizen soldiers not to fear because their faith made them mighty and their God was more powerful than their enemies. The Bible has over 350 verses that tell us to "Fear not," "Do not be afraid," "Do not worry," and "Be courageous." Other Scriptures describe how we can find peace amid fear-filled storms.

We face battles both in the external world and in our minds. These battles are intertwined, and the outcome of one affects the other. If fear gains control in our minds, it weakens our ability to protect ourselves in the world. However, maintaining focus can help us triumph over these internal battles. Nehemiah's reminder about the importance of courage for the sake of their families was a powerful call to action.

Protecting our family and livelihood gives us focus. Remembering that God is powerful and on our side in all his awesomeness gives us confidence. We need to continue fighting for our families.

The biblical story of Jesus walking on water is not just a miracle but a testament to the incredible power of faith. We may somewhat dismiss its significance because Jesus was God. Yet when we see Peter doing what Jesus did, we are filled with awe and inspiration, realizing the potential of our own faith. It can make miracles happen. However, if we waver in our faith by taking our focus off Jesus, we may experience trouble even worse than what we started with.

I did that. I was walking in faith, and then I took my eyes off Jesus for a minute, and I started sinking fast. This happened a couple of years after my twenty-two-year marriage ended, and I began dating again. I thought I was a rock-solid Christian who could handle anything. But I had vulnerable places when it came to rejection. When I took my eyes off Jesus to focus on finding a husband who would fill that hole in my life, I made some huge mistakes. I allowed myself to be led by the fear of being alone for the rest of my life. I quickly agreed to marry someone I didn't know well. The consequences were unimaginably devastating. I made many life-changing decisions without focusing on Jesus, and suddenly, I was in over my head, drowning.

The beautiful reality, though, is that Jesus still loved me. He pulled me out of that disaster and let me sit quietly with him while I regained my strength. He is the same God that Nehemiah claimed is great and awesome.

I learned the hard way to stay focused on Jesus. But now, my faith is strong enough to be thankful for the journey. Rebuilding is draining, hard, and sometimes overwhelming. Having the faith to focus on Jesus releases his power and authority over the enemy's attacks. Now, I can go into battle as a warrior with the backing of Jesus himself.

When the disciples saw him walking on the water, they were terrified. In their fear, they cried out, "It's a ghost!" But Jesus spoke to them at once. "Don't be afraid," he said. "Take courage. I am here!" Then Peter called to him, "Lord, if it's really you, tell me to come to you, walking on the water." "Yes, come," Jesus said. So Peter went over the side of the boat and walked on the water toward Jesus. But when he saw the strong wind and the waves, he was terrified and began to sink. "Save me, Lord!" he shouted. Jesus immediately reached out and grabbed him. "You have so little faith," Jesus said. "Why did you doubt me?" When they climbed back into the boat, the wind stopped.
Matthew 14:26–32 NLT

Lord, bless these readers with the courage to stay focused on you, even in the stormy seas of life. Peter showed us that if we focus intently, we can even walk on water! As we rebuild, we focus on you so that we will see miracles! *~In Jesus' name. Amen.*

Chapter 29

Keep Working

When our enemies heard that we were aware of their plot and that God had frustrated it, we all returned to the wall, each to our own work.
Nehemiah 4:15 NIV

Did you notice how Nehemiah refused to take credit for derailing their enemies' plots? He doesn't boast about how great his plan worked out or how perfectly he organized everything. No. He only gives credit to God and then goes back to the business of building walls.

To rebuild the walls, everyone needed to trust God and continue their work, even when danger was nearby. Nehemiah encouraged a mindset of relying on God's protection. He continued to remind the workers and their enemies that God was in charge of the project, and therefore, the walls would be rebuilt regardless of enemy attacks. So, the workers expected trouble, yet they could also have confidence.

Trouble was all around them, but they worked anyway. I like that. The workers were secure in trusting that the Lord was their protector. God's protection doesn't mean the attacks will stop or that we can drop our guard. It means that we effectively partner with God. The people do their part, and God does his part. God may frustrate all the enemy's evil plans, but we must still be prepared for the fight: We must be ready like any army, prepared to fight whether or not the battle enters our territory.

We are thirsty to learn about God when we start our faith journey. Different influences come along as the mountains and valleys of life change us. Life throws us curveballs that we are not ready for—unforeseen challenges with adverse outcomes that aren't part of our plans. How does my faith line up after life's disasters take their toll?

Others have told me that most people who have suffered experiences like mine will completely abandon God, and that is probably true. It's easy to run away when evil things happen. People often blame God for not protecting them or for allowing evil to exist in the world in the first place.

Part of the story of my dark time includes involvement with a church that ultimately turned out to be a cult. They gained credibility in my mind because of how much they truly loved Jesus—in an intense way that I had never seen before. Although their love for God was genuine, over time, they began to reveal so-called special revelations and secret teachings that were not biblical. They were very controlling and harsh to me and others in the fellowship. The leaders wove lies in with the truth of God. I looked to these people for help with the severe troubles and abuses in my marriage, but instead, they spiritually and emotionally abused me also. Their insensitive, controlling, and denigrating leadership led to the final battle that left me an utterly broken-down pile of rubble.

As I exited this horrible chapter of my life, I chose to dig into my relationship with God deeper than ever. At the point where many people would turn their backs on God, I decided to go all in. I would not let my fall become a victory for the enemy of my soul. Although I was going through another divorce, another move, and another job, I had a fresh new partnership with God.

The fact is, I did learn a lot from "that place" (which is what the other ex-members now call it). They baptized me in the Holy Spirit. This church was located in Israel, so I got to visit the Holy Land three times. I have seen the wall around Jerusalem with my own eyes. I even gained new perspectives, revelations, and a greater understanding of Scripture. While I also learned a lot about being spiritually deceived, ultimately, I became more mature in my faith—even though I learned it the hard way.

I became determined to dig deeper into the Word of God so I could understand the truth and recognize the lies. I had to develop a more significant partnership with the Holy Spirit to wade through the noise. People can justify false teaching by twisting a verse here and there, but if you want to know what God is saying, you must learn the Scriptures yourself and get help from the Holy Spirit. I thought I knew the Bible, but after being baptized in the Holy Spirit, the Word of God expanded exponentially and came alive in new ways. New layers of understanding were revealed, and it has been an exciting pursuit.

As I had just experienced with that cult, some people are driven by their own spirits or even *un*holy spirits, and they are off track. These people give Spirit-filled churches a bad reputation. Still, I can't throw away the influences of the Holy Spirit. I have experienced the gifts of the Spirit myself and assure you that they are alive and well in the world today. There is a healthy way to implement the gifts, so if you are in a confusing situation (like I was), keep seeking the truth until you find the right fit. The gifts are as necessary today as they ever were.

After God delivered me from that harmful situation, I kept working to know the truth in my heart. God continues to help me discern the truth within a comfort level that works for me, and I am finally learning where I fit into the body of Christ.

But this happened that we might not rely on ourselves but on God, who raises the dead. He has delivered us from such a deadly peril, and he will deliver us again. On him we have set our hope that he will continue to deliver us.
2 Corinthians 1:9–10 NIV

Father God, I pray for all the people reading this to find godly churches that nurture the gifts of the Spirit in healthy ways. Please give them the discernment needed to rightly evaluate where you want them and that they keep working through any problems until they find a good home. *~Amen.*

Chapter 30

Swords and Shields

From that day on, half of my men did the work, while the other half were equipped with spears, shields, bows, and armor... and each of the builders wore his sword at his side as he worked. But the man who sounded the trumpet stayed with me... So we continued the work with half the men holding spears, from the first light of dawn till the stars came out.
Nehemiah 4:16, 18, 21 NIV

What a team! They now had to assign half of the workers to guard duty, so they had to work long days to make substantial progress on the wall. The fear of attack was not going to stop the building project. These people worked together from dawn to dusk to get the job done and to protect the city at the same time. They had to be ready for battle constantly.

I personally don't know much about war or military operations, but I have learned much of what I do know by studying the Bible. Whether in competitions or battles, we always need two things for victory: defense and offense. Defensively, you put a strategy and weapons in place to protect yourself; offensively, you use weapons to harm the enemy before he harms you. Shields and armor protect the body from injury in battles as part of our personal protection and defenses. Sharp implements like arrows, spears, and swords were offensive weapons for combat during this time in history.

Nehemiah told the enemy they had weapons by positioning armed men around the construction. Even the workers had swords...just in case.

Many years ago, a friend lent me a CD series of messages about the armor of God. I tried listening to the teachings and couldn't connect with them. I couldn't absorb the information then, which was unusual for me. I had no fundamental understanding of the depth and importance of this Scripture passage, so I ignored the opportunity to learn about it. Yet the truth is, God doesn't tell us to put on armor for no reason—He knows we will face battles. He knew I needed that armor to face specific attacks coming at me, and I missed a God-given opportunity to prepare myself. The consequence was losing a battle before it started because I wasn't aware I needed to protect myself.

My defenses had been walls of self-accomplishment, career, and knowledge, but I didn't have a firm foundation because I established my defenses in fear and pride. These walls of fake protection didn't shield me from the fiery arrows attempting to take me down. They couldn't prepare me for a spiritual battle.

What kind of defenses does God want us to use? The armor of God has five pieces of defensive protection and one offensive weapon. There are many great teachings about this topic, so I'll quickly give you an overview that would have helped me.

- **Belt of truth**: The old King James language uses the phrase "girding our loins" with truth because when everyone wore tunics, you had to gather up the fabric with a belt to run in battle. Belts symbolize holding everything together. Holding onto God's truth increases our discernment and helps us make better decisions.

- **Breastplate of righteousness:** A breastplate protects the heart. The physical heart gives life to our body, but we also have a spiritual heart. Our heart includes our minds, emotions, feelings, motivations, and desires. Our heart is the very core of who we are as a person. When I left my heart unprotected, I paid a high price because I focused on worldly desires instead of right living. I didn't ask God what to do; I let my emotions drive my decisions, and I learned the hard way the value of protecting my heart.

- **Shoes fitted with the gospel of peace:** Shoes protect our feet, and our feet take us where we want to go. I had previously walked into situations without God, but later, I found more and more peace by walking with him instead. Shoes symbolize stability as we navigate life with the gospel that brings peace. I'll take some of that.

- **Shield of faith:** Effective shields protect the body, but we must also protect our souls. Faith is the primary mechanism by which we do that. Not self-importance. Not position. Not money. Not family. Not ego, fear, control, luck, weapons, intimidation, position, possessions, lifestyle, or anything that rises above our faith in God. None of those make long-term shields.

- **Helmet of salvation:** This is imagery for protecting our minds and our thought lives. Ideologies that counter everything God has for us bombard us every day, and they are getting worse very quickly. Our salvation and relationship with God must be at the core of our worldview. If not, our thoughts will be led by fears, lusts, and ambitions that carry us in adverse directions.

- **Sword of the Spirit:** When we put on the armor of God, several pieces protect us, and some prepare us for battle, but only one is an offensive weapon: the sword of the Spirit, which is the Word of God. The Word of God is essential. To win in spiritual warfare, we must know the words and strategies of God so we can pull them out and use them when we need to. The Word must become part of our nature so we can use it to cut down our enemy, the evil of this world.

So much is written about the armor of God, and my summary here is minuscule. Please don't ignore it like I did. My warfare has been successful when I armor up, but it fails when I don't.

Stand firm then, with the belt of truth buckled around your waist, with the breastplate of righteousness in place, and with your feet fitted with the readiness that comes from the gospel of peace. In addition to all this, take up the shield of faith, with which you can extinguish all the flaming arrows of the evil one. Take the helmet of salvation and the sword of the Spirit, which is the word of God.
Ephesians 6:14–17 NIV

God, you outfit everyone reading this with the equipment needed to be victorious in battle, but we decide if we want to wear it. I pray for them to recognize the importance of this passage and apply this wisdom to their daily approach to life. *~Amen.*

Chapter 31

Hunger

Now the men and their wives raised a great outcry against their fellow Jews. Some were saying, "We and our sons and daughters are numerous; in order for us to eat and stay alive, we must get grain." Others were saying, "We are mortgaging our fields, our vineyards and our homes to get grain during the famine."
Nehemiah 5:1–3 NIV

Now, a new problem was affecting the city: a food shortage. A famine could completely wipe out a community back in those days. After exhausting their supplies, they would have to buy food from other cities or countries, but the global economy wasn't transporting goods back and forth like we are used to today. Nehemiah realized the food suppliers were partners with the enemies. Those enemies now had more control over the situation by manipulating food prices and availability. This story records how people mortgaged everything to buy food to live.

A season of hunger changes how we live. Our first instinct is to deal with it privately, figuring out a few ways to earn extra cash. We may refinance our house or car. If it worsens, we may move to a less expensive home or take money out of our retirement fund. When we become more desperate, we go public and ask for help from others or the government.

For those rebuilding the walls of Jerusalem, hunger complicated matters and changed their priorities—it is essential to keep people fed. Their most basic need was the ingredients needed to make bread. Grain, oil, yeast, and salt became the new focus of their lives as these staples were critical to the entire community's survival.

Several times during his brief ministry here on earth, Jesus said, "I am the bread of life." He talked a lot about the necessities of life: food, farming, cooking, etc. To that audience, these were the essentials for physical life two thousand years ago. It's fascinating how Jesus used the everyday activities of his time to demonstrate God's powerful spiritual principles that are still easily understood today.

Some of Jesus' most famous miracles showed how he could satisfy the basic physical need for food. During his walk on earth, Jesus fed thousands of people with just two fish and five loaves of bread. Even today, his provision fills our stomachs. But he also nourishes our souls and feeds our spiritual beings.

I don't like going a day without food, and I don't do well without spiritual food every day either. If I treat Jesus like a birthday cake that I only enjoy on special occasions, then he is not a basic necessity in my life. Some people only attend church on holidays. Some only think about God for an hour on Sundays, and that's it. They think that's enough of Jesus. I can't do that. I am hungrier than that.

Here is a recipe for staying spiritually full every day:

- **Devour the Word of God:** I've learned to love studying the Bible.
  Jesus answered, "It is written: 'Man shall not live on bread alone, but on every word that comes from the mouth of God.'" Matthew 4:4 NIV

- **Worship and praise,** including giving thanks for my many blessings. I find things to be grateful for and often reflect on the very last verse of the Psalms:
  Let everything that has breath praise the LORD. Praise the LORD! Psalms 150:6 NKJV

- **Pray** for my family, friends, enemies, ministry, church family, job, finances, home, daily needs, faith, and future. I also love praying in tongues because you can do it without any mental effort.

So what shall I do? I will pray with my spirit, but I will also pray with my understanding; I will sing with my spirit, but I will also sing with my understanding. 1 Corinthians 14:15 NIV

- **Forgive others and repent for my sin.** One of the best disciplines I've learned from the twelve-step program is to take a daily inventory and immediately admit my wrongs. And forgive us our debts, as we also have forgiven our debtors. Matthew 6:12 NIV

- **Pursue deliverance and healing.** Many problems result from opening doors to the enemy, so get rid of them and close the doors. Stop giving the enemy access. Stop believing his lies. And lead us not into temptation, but deliver us from the evil one. Matthew 6:13 NIV

- **Declare the good things that God says about me!** Repeating God's promises reinforces a personal relationship with him. You will also declare a thing, And it will be established for you; So light will shine on your ways. Job 22:28 NKJV

- **Listen to what God is telling me.** It is a good practice to journal, write, or creatively express the messages we hear from God. My sheep hear My voice, and I know them, and they follow Me. John 10:27 NKJV

"The true bread of God is the one who comes down from heaven and gives life to the world." "Sir," they said, "give us that bread every day." Jesus replied, "I am the bread of life. Whoever comes to me will never be hungry again. Whoever believes in me will never be thirsty. John 6:33–35 NLT

Jesus, you are what our souls are hungry for, and I pray for us to crave even more of you, the Bread of Life. *~Amen.*

Chapter 32

Strongholds

When I heard their outcry and these charges, I was very angry. I pondered them in my mind and then accused the nobles and officials. I told them, "You are charging your own people interest!" So I called together a large meeting to deal with them.
Nehemiah 5:6–7 NIV

Nehemiah discovered that people in his community were taking advantage of the famine, placing even greater burdens on the hungry workers by charging them interest. It was bad enough that the people were going hungry, but to his disgust, he discovered that wealthier leaders were using the famine to their advantage.

The leaders in the community profited from the misfortune of others. Nehemiah expected different behavior from God's people, but the reality is that even God's loved ones are influenced by how the rest of the world thinks. What happened with these loans in Jerusalem may not have *seemed* wrong because charging interest on loans is standard business practice. However, when you are charging interest to your hungry brothers and sisters, it's a different situation. They thought of it like any business transaction, but in a famine, you may need to break that stronghold of human reasoning and take care of your people.

As usual, we see Nehemiah dealing with the people's behavior in ways we can learn from. He calls out the truth by exposing the predatory actions of wealthy citizens—without sugarcoating their behavior. Nehemiah shines a light on a dark situation, revealing the truth. He first talks to the nobles and officials and then calls for a meeting.

A spiritual stronghold is a fortress in our mind, a thought process built up to protect us. We have some positive ones, but we also have many negative ones. The best stronghold we can have is God himself. His protective guardrails help us stay on the right road. The strongholds of human reasoning are the logical thought processes we learn from the world. They can derail us from pursuing God because their source is rooted in the Tree of Knowledge of Good and Evil rather than the Tree of Life (Genesis 2–3).

We have already discussed how I built fear-based strongholds aligned with the world's lies: "divorce is normal," "success means more money," and "sexual encounters are love." I believed these messages in my heart because my mother repeatedly told me, "You will never be able to count on a man to take care of you." Her words built a stronghold in me and convinced me to expect rejection.

Let's analyze this further. Why do any of us believe the lies? Events in life cause pain, anger, bitterness, shame, misery, rejection, grief, and confusion. Some of our ungodly strongholds resulted from outright trauma, yet another source can be from dysfunction that seemed normal because it's just how our home life operated.

Family dysfunction can often be a clue about the effects of generational sin. Alcoholism in my family is a notable example. I was saved long before I began drinking every day. I got baptized and studied the Bible regularly. I was attending church and was even involved in ministry, but my drinking escalated, just like it did for my father and his father before him. Because I didn't realign all my thinking, my behaviors began to override the freedom Jesus provided and gave the devil an open door to harass me. I believed what the world said about moderation, and before I knew it, I couldn't stop. I eventually chose to break the stronghold and dismantle the comfort cycles that supported it. It turns out that I didn't need a drink just because it was five o'clock!

The apostle Paul was talking to Christians when he said to knock down the strongholds of human reasoning. He then says to take our thoughts captive and make them obedient to Jesus Christ. This is how we get free.

Here is how to tear down negative strongholds:

- Identify the stronghold: Ask the Holy Spirit to show you the lie you have embraced. Strongholds are often associated with fear, guilt from the past, or family dysfunction.

- Now, ask the Holy Spirit to show you how that lie originated in your life.

- Repent for believing the lie and begin dealing with the issue's roots. Sincere repentance closes the door on the stronghold.

Renew your mind as follows:

- Ask the Holy Spirit to show you the truth. Meditate on his answers, which may involve researching that topic in the Bible.

- Believe the truth and exercise your will to choose his ways over the world's human reasoning. Sometimes, that requires repeating the truth aloud multiple times daily for at least twenty-one days. This is called neuroplasticity[1], which is a scientifically proven way to retrain our thoughts and rewire our brains (renew our minds).

- Fill your emptiness with the Holy Spirit instead of the false comforts of the world.

God has a better way to destroy the ineffective walls that defy the world's logic. Following the strategies above helps us rebuild ourselves in God's way, bringing true freedom and victory in removing the rubble in our lives.

We use God's mighty weapons, not worldly weapons, to knock down the strongholds of human reasoning and to destroy false arguments. We destroy every proud obstacle that keeps people from knowing God. We capture their rebellious thoughts and teach them to obey Christ.
2 Corinthians 10:4–5 NLT

Heavenly Father, I pray for everyone digging in to eradicate strongholds. I pray for them to discover your truths and find freedom as old strongholds are destroyed, and healthy strongholds are created. *~Amen.*

Chapter 33

Debts

"You must restore their fields, vineyards, olive groves, and homes to them this very day. And repay the interest you charged when you lent them money, grain, new wine, and olive oil." They replied, "We will give back everything and demand nothing more from the people. We will do as you say." Then I called the priests and made the nobles and officials swear to do what they had promised.
Nehemiah 5:11–12 NLT

The wealthy nobles were aggravating the community's hardships during the famine by charging interest on their loans. Nehemiah reminded them of their responsibility and realigned them to support one another. Their unity had eroded due to the corrupt desires of a few elite individuals; a situation Nehemiah was determined to rectify.

Nehemiah's rebuke went beyond calling out greed. He persuaded the bankers to forgive the debts and swear an oath, a solemn promise to the priests, the people, and God that they would never again impose such loans. It was a tangible step toward acknowledging their mistakes and committing to a better future.

The most profound change we witness in this passage is the officials' decision to forgive all the debt and return their profits. This act ensured everyone had the resources to weather the famine together, strengthening their commitment to support each other. Forgiving debt was a powerful tool to reset the community's course, as the loans were inherently unethical.

It feels great to pay off a debt. While struggling financially, I made the final payment on my car and experienced an enormous difference in my stress level. Eventually, I could also pay off all the debt I racked up due to my poor decisions, and I finally had some breathing room in my finances.

But I had a more significant debt that I could never pay off by myself—the heavy debt of my sin. This was a massive pile of rubble, and I would never have been able to clean it up. I can't do enough good to outweigh the wrongs that I am responsible for, so I'm thankful that Jesus paid for my debt of sin at the cross. He paid to redeem me, and now I want a life that reflects the extravagant love that he showed me.

Jesus taught the importance of both sides of forgiving debts: being forgiven and forgiving others. Jesus told a parable about a king who completely forgave one of his servants for a debt equivalent to a million dollars (Matthew 18:21–35). This parable is a metaphor for the debt of our sins. But there's another part to that story. After the king showed mercy by forgiving the enormous debt, that same servant turned around and threw a coworker into debtors' prison for a thousand-dollar debt. His actions showed that he still didn't understand mercy, and his heart was still wicked even though he experienced forgiveness himself. He never allowed the forgiveness he had received to penetrate his heart and remained unchanged by the king's generosity.

Just before he tells this parable, Jesus says that we should forgive others seventy times seven times, meaning we should be unlimited in our forgiveness. Forgiveness is a foundational Christian principle, and our goals should include that same mercy, love, and generosity to others.

I can choose to be changed by the generosity of King Jesus or not. When I model the forgiveness given to me, I walk on the path to freedom in the kingdom of God. If my attitude toward others doesn't change, it's like I climbed back into the rubble, rebuilding the old walls of resentment, offense, anger, bitterness, and unhappiness.

When I let go of retaliation and my need to teach them a lesson, I allow God to do his job instead of trying to do it for him. I can guard my heart and move on without carrying the heavy bricks of bitterness.

Touched by his plea, the king let him off, erasing the debt.
Matthew 18:27 MSG

Heavenly Father, thank you for modeling how we should approach forgiving others. I'm praying that all the readers of this message find freedom through forgiving others so that no one is stuck in the prison of unforgiveness. *~In Jesus' name. Amen.*

Chapter 34

Different

But the earlier governors—those preceding me—placed a heavy burden on the people and took forty shekels of silver from them in addition to food and wine. Their assistants also lorded it over the people. But out of reverence for God I did not act like that. Furthermore, a hundred and fifty Jews and officials ate at my table, as well as those who came to us from the surrounding nations.
Nehemiah 5:15, 17 NIV

During this time, Nehemiah had the honor of serving as the governor of Jerusalem, and many privileges came with that position. Back then, the governors and officials were allowed to impose extra taxes on the people so that they could live in luxury. Nehemiah did the opposite and was generous with his food and home. He was different from the other governors and walked in the ways of God instead of the ways of man.

In God's kingdom economy, there is order, hierarchy, respect, and honor for the leadership placed over the people. Nehemiah refused to take advantage of his position because he considered himself a representative of God to the people he was governing. Nehemiah approached his job with excellence and trustworthiness, not expecting favors or special treatment. He was different and didn't take advantage of the community by taxing them to support a life of privilege, even though that was culturally acceptable.

I am different now.

Who I am today is not the same person I was before. The difference is measurable. For example, I was classified as an extrovert on personality assessments I previously took for work. However, I now test as an introvert or sometimes as an ambivert, which crosses between those characteristics. This kind of assessment helps us understand how we interact with the rest of the world, and I think it is interesting that my experiences changed that particular trait.

Life happened. It affected how I see the world, react to people, and what I'm interested in. I still do many activities with people. I'm not isolating; I simply don't seek attention like I used to. I have more friends right now than I've ever had, but I no longer feel the need to be the star of the show.

When I first got sober, I earnestly began the process of putting on my new nature. This commitment took my spiritual walk to a new level. Until then, I approached Christianity with an academic understanding rather than deep personal application. I knew the Bible intellectually but didn't truly live it out. I wanted more.

Our walk as a Christian follows a typical progression. We begin attending church on Sunday mornings or listening to online teachings. Then, we start reading the Bible, which eventually becomes an everyday routine. Along the way, we add prayer to the mix. That's a great foundation yet it leaves many of us in that state of Christian hypocrisy people complain about. I was like that for many years. I was a Christian who was taking the right actions but still hanging on to my old ways. My faith was still mixed with the ways of the world. I transformed some of my life while still holding onto walls of protection and comfort. We can indeed be saved and not transformed. Being saved is a choice. Being renewed and transformed is another series of choices. Becoming different is a choice.

God loves us wherever we are on the journey and gives us grace along the way. We become different the more we live in obedience. That's when we start making more significant leaps and are set free. For me, getting sober was a major step. Learning to be filled with the Holy Spirit was another huge leap.

 I began stripping away my pride and fear a little at a time. I started saying no to some of my poor choices. Yes, I am still working on many areas—we are all works in progress—but I have made significant changes that have genuinely made me different. I'm thankful that God renews my thoughts and attitudes as I progressively immerse myself in his nature. The King James Bible translation says this is taking off our old man and putting on the new man God wants for us.

I'm probably not as fun as I used to be. I'm much more focused on Jesus. I don't speak as assertively, and don't blend in very well in some social situations. I am very focused on my spiritual development and more interested in spiritual maturity than most people. But I'm okay with that.

Throw off your old sinful nature and your former way of life, which is corrupted by lust and deception. Instead, let the Spirit renew your thoughts and attitudes. Put on your new nature, created to be like God—truly righteous and holy.
Ephesians 4:22–24 NLT

God, I pray that we will all be motivated to throw off our old ways, a little at a time, as the Holy Spirit leads us to renew our thoughts and become more like you every day. *~In Jesus' name. ~Amen.*

Chapter 35

Devoted

Instead, I devoted myself to the work on this wall. All my men were assembled there for the work; we did not acquire any land. Remember me with favor, my God, for all I have done for these people.
Nehemiah 5:16, 19 NIV

The dictionary defines *devotion* as "giving all or a large part of one's time or resources."[1] Not only did Nehemiah devote himself to building the wall, but everyone in town also made it their highest priority. Building the wall could only happen if everyone stayed committed to the project.

The work on the wall kept many people from earning a living doing their regular jobs. With economic activity at a standstill, many in the community were probably very tempted to return to their routine work. But the wall was growing, and everyone was committed to finishing the rebuilding project together. As they got closer to completion, it was apparent how God was blessing the work.

Though the project was progressing and the end was in sight, the people had to continue prioritizing the wall. Returning to your other projects becomes tempting when you have made steady headway and can see the finish line. The final push to completion can sometimes be the most challenging part of the journey, so staying devoted to the effort is critical as the end nears.

And God honored Nehemiah's request to be remembered for this project. God named a whole book in the Bible after him, and people like me are inspired by looking at Nehemiah's accomplishments.

Okay, people. If Nehemiah is almost done building the wall, then I must be almost done writing my book. I want to move on to the next stage, but there are seventeen chapters remaining. That feels like a lot. Thankfully, I know many wonderful topics are ahead, which keep me motivated.

I'm not just *thinking* about writing a book; I'm doing it. I want it to be the best it can be, and I want people to read it and be motivated and excited to work on their rubble. I am going to be devoted to this book until it is published. I am a finisher.

I was devoted to working on my mess for a long time. I called it my season of healing. I studied the Bible intently. I went through *many* freedom programs. I read lots of books and watched hundreds of sermons and teachings. I completed the worksheets, inventories, and checklists. I went through many inner healing and deliverance sessions. I said thousands of declarations and decrees. I learned what God says about me because I won't spend my life hating myself or being bitter. I wanted to overcome my victim mentality, and that takes work. I trusted that God had remarkable plans ahead if I stayed devoted to my journey toward healing and maturity.

Each thing I worked on was one more brick on the road to freedom—one more brick and then another. Some were heavy, and some just needed to be moved off the pile of rubble and cleared out of the way.

My season of healing lasted several years, and then God directed me to step up to a greater level of serving. I had to start focusing on others (instead of myself) and applying what I was learning. Healing never ends, but God wanted me to start serving others. For me, that meant leading and mentoring women in my recovery community. That was a fantastic time of growth for me—and them.

And now I'm in the season of sharing. I have wanted to write my entire life, and now my freedom story is being brought to life. So here we are.

**Let perseverance finish its work so that you may be mature and complete,
not lacking anything.**
James 1:4 NIV

Jesus, you showed us what it is like to stick with an objective. Through you, we can finish everything needed to be mature followers. I pray now that everyone working on their path to freedom will be devoted to your promptings along the way. ~*Amen.*

Chapter 36

Discerning

Sanballat and Geshem sent me this message: "Come, let us meet together in one of the villages on the plain of Ono." But they were scheming to harm me; so I sent messengers to them with this reply: "I am carrying on a great project and cannot go down. Why should the work stop while I leave it and go down to you?" Four times they sent me the same message, and each time I gave them the same answer.
Nehemiah 6:2–4 NIV

In Nehemiah's story, the bad guys were constantly scheming to oppose and create trouble for this project. Once again, we find them trying to shut down the rebuilding. They failed to invade the city, so now they tried to lure Nehemiah away from town to do him in. Thankfully, Nehemiah was anointed and equipped for his unique work, and he could see through their schemes and discern trouble in their meeting request.

Even though the project was nearing completion, the opposition was still a problem, and their new plan was to ambush Nehemiah. Their plots had previously included all kinds of threats against the city, and now the enemies were spreading rumors about Nehemiah and trying to entrap him.

Nehemiah correctly discerned the scheming spirit behind the enemy's request and used discerning wisdom in his response. He didn't waste his time with political games and wasn't willing to risk his objective for a wild goose chase with people proven to be against the restoration of the wall around Jerusalem. Nehemiah kept the project as his highest priority and gave his adversaries a firm no.

The New Testament discusses two kinds of discernment: one is a gift from the Holy Spirit, and the other comes from the wisdom of knowing the Word of God in our hearts. We need both kinds of discernment. Nehemiah had both. I want both, too.

People often think of the spiritual gift mentioned in 1 Corinthians 12:10 as general discernment and perceptive wisdom, but that is not what the gift describes. The spiritual gift mentioned is the discerning *of spirits*. In many modern Bible versions, such as the NASB, this Greek word is translated as *distinguishing* of spirits, which may be a better term. The spiritual gift refers to a supernatural ability to understand whether a situation operates from the Holy Spirit, an evil spirit, or our fleshly nature. This gift from God helps us know how to respond correctly.

A word study in the New Testament on *discernment* uncovers that general discernment is rooted in knowledge and insight—that is, knowledge of love, God, and biblical truth. Spiritual maturity brings this, which we need when faced with the world's schemes. Bringing these two types of discernment together helps us respond wisely to the world's attacks as Nehemiah did.

As I spiritually matured and grew in both kinds of discernment, I've (generally) made better decisions. I have become wiser and more open to the things of God, as well as discerning the spiritual forces at work. I still make some wrong decisions, but as I grow, I can see those motives more clearly and am more aware of the forces affecting my choices than I used to be. This helps me hear the voice of God more clearly over my own thoughts.

I now see how much fear has driven my decisions and behaviors. Because I was afraid of rejection, I created a hard shell to make people (including me) think I was strong and confident. Being impulsive, outgoing, pushy, loud, and taking risks was part of that facade. It has taken time to uncover the roots of these attributes. Things that helped include emotional healing and becoming more rooted in the Word. By dismantling those structures, I have been better equipped to use the gifts of the Spirit to direct my life. Spiritual discernment gives me the perspective of responding to life more effectively.

And this I pray, that your love may overflow still more and more in real
knowledge and all discernment, so that you may discover the things that
are excellent, that you may be sincere
and blameless for the day of Christ.
Philippians 1:9–10

Father God, you have given us your Holy Spirit and many spiritual gifts to help us navigate the challenges and temptations of this life. Strengthen, empower, and enlighten all of us to use your gifts, love, and knowledge as our foundation going forward. *~Amen.*

Chapter 37

Strength

For all of them were trying to frighten us, thinking, "They will become discouraged with the work and it will not be done."
But now, God, strengthen my hands.
Nehemiah 6:9

Ongoing harassment can make us feel weak and discouraged. Even Nehemiah could get discouraged. But he knew enough to pray for strength. When external stresses produce a hard and weary season of life, we may need encouragement beyond what we can muster ourselves.

We have built-in mechanisms for rest and renewal. We need food every few hours and sleep every night. Downtime and rest are requirements of living, but even that is not always enough. When we experience an extended period of stress or exertion, our fountain of strength may run dry, and we may have no choice but to ask for help. Nehemiah reminds us to ask God for more strength to endure demanding times. It's hard to admit that we aren't strong enough to do everything, but engaging our spiritual strength often leads to renewed physical strength.

Life. It comes at us in waves of remarkable growth and waves of difficulty, in floods of joy and torrents of tragedy, in surges of fun and seasons of demanding work. None of us has the choice of a steady, problem-free life where we cruise along. In nature, plants need adversity so their roots can grow deep and strong. Growth through adversity has been the source of many sermons because we need God's strength to overcome the challenges.

Times of difficulty often catch us by surprise. For example, when my mom died. I was only thirty-six and was unprepared for the changes that loss brought to me and my family. I quit my corporate job to take over a small business that my mom had started. I unexpectedly became an entrepreneur when that was never on my radar. I suddenly had an unpredictable income and worked from home long before that was popular. I learned entirely new skills. The transition was hard, and my faith grew incrementally as my family adapted. These challenges were all within the range of normal life changes we all experience over time.

A more challenging season of change was when I remarried at the age of fifty-five. Life quickly went from the excitement of being with someone new to the stark reality of being in an abusive marriage that required me to learn how to tolerate, pretend, protect, deflect, and hide. I had to adapt. I had to dig a deeper foundation to keep me grounded because I needed strength I didn't have on my own. I needed supernatural strength.

In these two examples, I needed different levels of faith to navigate the challenging times of change. When my mom died, I could rely on previous experiences, friends, family, and personal motivation to adapt to the unexpected changes. I needed God's help, but I didn't *desperately* depend on him like I did during that life-crushing season of marriage. In the latter situation, I only had God to lean on.

God may not send difficulties our way to teach us lessons, but he does use those situations to bring out his precious gifts and allow us to lean on him in new ways. An atheist friend of mine once said they don't believe in God because they don't need a crutch. When I had foot surgery, I was very thankful to have support for my body while my foot was healing. It would not be able to grow strong if I walked on it. A crutch was essential for the healing process, so I could become stronger. Likewise, using God as my crutch in tough times was a lifesaver.

Growing in faith is a choice. Many people walk away from God entirely and question his goodness when they experience hardship. But we all go through hardship. Some of these are a natural part of life, like a parent dying. Some difficulties are the consequences of our own choices. Some are the results of evil decisions made by other people. Some are spiritual attacks. In all of these, we can grow in resilience and faith. We can ask God for strength and be amazed at what he provides.

I know what it is to be in need, and I know what it is to have plenty. I have learned the secret of being content in any and every situation, whether well fed or hungry, whether living in plenty or in want. I can do all this through him who gives me strength.
Philippians 4:12–13 NIV

Lord Jesus, you provide the secrets of contentment and strength to get through anything. Help us receive your strength during every hardship we need to overcome. Thank you for being our strength as we heal. ~*Amen.*

Chapter 38

Betrayed

But I said, "Should a man like me flee? And who is there like me who
would go into the temple to save his own life? I will not go in." Then I
realized that God certainly had not sent him,
but he uttered his prophecy against me because
Tobiah and Sanballat had hired him.
Nehemiah 6:11–12

One of the townspeople tried to convince Nehemiah to hide in
the temple to avoid being killed by Tobiah and Sanballat, but Nehemiah discerned it was a setup. The strategy of this new plot was
to portray Nehemiah as a coward and undermine his credibility.
So, there he was, betrayed by one of his own people.

This story shows how relentless enemies can be. These bad
guys had tried every avenue to kill or discredit Nehemiah. The
enemies, led by Tobiah and Sanballat, were willing to endanger
the whole city by ruining the project and this man of integrity.
They were now taking their attacks to a new and more personal
level: betrayal.

Betrayal can cause deeply rooted bitterness and even create
identity issues. Nehemiah discerned more about the situation
than what was on the surface. He immediately saw it as just another attack from his ever-present enemies, and he wasn't willing to
take it personally. Nehemiah perceived that a paid, faithless mid-
dleman was being used to trap him. However, our hero continued
his outstanding leadership by staying on task so they could finish
the wall.

A betrayal blindsided me during my healing journey. I was successfully taking my pile of rubble and building my path toward freedom, and then, *boom*, it happened. I was hit with a betrayal that rocked me to the core. The people involved probably never knew how deeply their actions impacted me because they were dealing with the rubble falling on their side of the wall. At the time, my betrayers suffered significantly more damage than I did. Nonetheless, I reeled from this betrayal—from my friends—for quite a while. I had never experienced anything like it. The betrayal included lying, sin, and broken trust, so I cut ties and took my pain to the Lord. This hurt was utterly unexpected, and my heart ached.

I had been practicing my newfound skills in godly forgiveness, but this was different. How could I forgive this? I didn't know if I even wanted to. I had already forgiven so much. Especially at first, I didn't want to deal with this new betrayal. Maybe I could deal with it later.

I've learned much about forgiving and know that unforgiveness blocks my relationship with the Lord. Unforgiveness would keep me in bondage, and my goal was freedom.

I took a closer look at how Jesus was betrayed. He knew it would happen, yet he didn't stop it. His betrayer was someone close to him. Someone he had loved and cared about. Someone on his team, one of his disciples. Meditating on this helped me process betrayal, which was minuscule compared to what happened to Jesus. His betrayal led to torture and death. My torture was self-inflicted. Once again, I should have known better.

Jesus showed us a lifestyle of forgiveness and taught us about it multiple times. Even hanging on the cross, Jesus forgave those involved in his arrest and crucifixion. I want this kind of love to permeate my being and flow from me.

I knew that forgiving from my heart would eliminate the bitterness that could come from my wounds. I eventually yielded my heart in this area to Jesus, who is the forgiver. Repenting for my *wrong responses* was part of the process. Forgiving others is part of God's plan, but that doesn't transform our betrayers into safe people. It doesn't mean I have to stay in contact with them.

The betrayal still hurts a bit, indicating that I need to forgive them more. I still grieve some over the lost trust. When healing is complete, I can say goodbye to resentment. Goodbye, bitterness. Hello, freedom.

And as they were eating, He said, "Truly I say to you that one of you will betray Me." Being deeply grieved, they began saying to Him, each one: "Surely it is not I, Lord?"
Matthew 26:21–22

Lord, betrayal can trigger so many emotions, and I pray for every reader who needs to overcome this kind of hurt. I pray for the ability to see their own negative reactions, for the determination to forgive, and for the grieving process associated with any necessary relationship changes. *~In Jesus' name, Amen.*

Chapter 39

Finished

The wall was finished on the twenty-fifth day of Elul.
It had taken fifty-two days.
Nehemiah 6:15 MSG

The wall was complete, and the city could move forward with confidence and security. Through their focused efforts, the workers finished the project in fifty-two days. Imagine that! Only fifty-two days. They rebuilt a wall almost forty feet tall, eight feet wide, two and a half miles long, with ten gates. That's a lot of rocks to move around in two months. What a fantastic accomplishment!

Everyone in town participated in building a magnificent and significant wall. This monumental undertaking could only be achieved by a large, well-coordinated team blessed by God himself. While we acknowledge Nehemiah for his outstanding leadership, his project account also shows that he continuously credited the families and people, the laborers doing the work. He appreciated the efforts of everyone involved.

Nehemiah and the people built an enduring wall that lasted until 70 AD when the Romans destroyed Jerusalem. They leveled the entire city, including the temple and the city wall. The wall was rebuilt in the 1500s, which is what we see around the city today.

The legacy of Nehemiah's project lives on because he journaled about it. His records are in the Bible and are still used today as an example of leadership and teamwork.

The wall might be complete, but the story isn't over yet. Like most significant projects, the project involved several steps to completion: a rollout process, a training period, and finally, a big launch party.

When he went to the cross, Jesus declared, "It is finished," as he completed his earthly ministry. But that wasn't the end of the story. If that were all there was, we wouldn't even consider Jesus to be God. The unexpected game changer came next in the story: the resurrection. Then, it got even better: the release of the Holy Spirit.

As with everything in life, one season finishes, and another begins.

For me, "It is finished" means "freedom begins" because I now have the supernatural resurrection power of the Holy Spirit living in me. I need his help. His power. His direction. The goal of Christianity is to love God and others, to be unoffendable, to find contentment in all circumstances, and to grow in the fruit of the Spirit: love, joy, peace, patience, kindness, goodness, faithfulness, gentleness, and self-control (Galatians 5:22–23). We need the Holy Spirit to do that because we can't do it alone.

Jesus came to set the captives free, and freedom is a process. Authentic freedom and healing don't come from just knowing *about* Jesus. We need the Holy Spirit to help us grab as much of that freedom as we are willing to pursue. Our faith is a progression, a maturity, that moves from just believing in Jesus to accepting him as our Savior and ultimately making him Lord of our lives. Even the apostles, who walked with Jesus in his earthly life and knew him personally, didn't realize there was more to come. After Jesus' resurrection, they were given the Holy Spirit (John 20:22), but there was still even more to come. On the day of Pentecost, they were baptized in the Holy Spirit and received powerful boldness.

Little by little, we release the grip the world has on our thinking and receive more of what God has for us. We align with the peace and freedom of walking with the Holy Spirit. We can grow in increasingly more freedom, which includes the following:

- understanding the power and authority of believers in Jesus Christ

- using the armor of God to overcome evil

- believing our identity in Christ

- renewing our minds

- hearing from God and knowing his will

- accepting and giving forgiveness

- and so much more!

Once I started learning about these concepts, I couldn't stop incorporating them into my life because they changed me. They made me a better person. They helped deepen my relationship with God. Eventually, I even experienced freedom from most of the stronghold thinking that kept me feeling unloved and stuck in a victim mentality.

Therefore when Jesus had received the sour wine, He said, "It is finished!"
And He bowed His head and gave up His spirit.
John 19:30

Jesus, your finished work on the cross left us with the most powerful gift of all: the Holy Spirit. May your gifts continue to bless those of us working through our piles of rubble and set us free! ~ *Amen.*

Chapter 40

Miracles

When all our enemies heard about it, and all the nations surrounding us saw it, they lost their confidence; for they realized that this work had been accomplished with the help of our God.
Nehemiah 6:16

The enemies probably never imagined the wall could be finished in such a short time. They were expecting to have many opportunities to attack and undermine the rebuilding taking place in Jerusalem. One thing they didn't factor into their plan was supernatural help. When a project is commissioned and blessed by God himself, there will be no way to fathom its greatness, no way to expect what is coming, and no way to explain it. This is what we call a miracle.

When we hear about something that exceeds man's capabilities, we may have to accept that more is going on than meets the eye. Throughout history, events that don't fit within the laws of nature or the known framework of how life operates have occurred. Rebuilding a protective wall around a city in fifty-two days is one of those indescribable miracles.

The unexpected completion of the wall filled everyone who heard about it with fear because they understood it was a message about God's power and authority over this project. The universe around us is full of unexplainable things that fill us with awe, wonder, and respect for God's miraculous capabilities.

I *loved* wine. I *really enjoyed* a good margarita. And after a stressful day at work, there was nothing like the calming effect of a brandy old-fashioned (yes, I lived in Wisconsin). But the enemy is sneaky. Initially, I just enjoyed these drinks occasionally, but before I knew it, I couldn't get through a day without them. They became my comfort on bad days, my reward on good days, and my coping mechanism every day. Eventually, a time came when I *had* to have a drink every day. I couldn't stop. And I didn't know how to stop.

Some people can't relate to my experience with alcohol, but they can relate to standing in front of the pantry looking for something salty after just binging on something sweet. Or maybe trying not to look at that naughty website. Or maybe vowing to have just one final cigarette and then no more, ever. Or spending the day gripped in depression or fear. Or playing one more online game. Or excusing another abusive attack because you are sure it will never happen again. Or not being able to stop the pain pills after the injury from an accident. Many types of addictions can unexpectedly overtake us. And then, we're stuck.

I had tried to quit drinking several times on my own, but it never worked. In fact, the opposite happened; the more I tried to stop drinking, the more I drank. I had to come to the point where I was willing to get help, and I finally walked through the doors of Celebrate Recovery. I started working through my addictive drinking issues, and I got sober.

It turned out that I needed the wisdom of other people to accomplish what I couldn't do on my own. When I broke down and sought help in a Christian recovery program, I met a bunch of walking miracles—people who had overcome their hurts, habits, and hangups with the help of Jesus. They were like me, and for the first time in my life, I was part of a community of Jesus-loving people who showed unconditional love to everyone who walked through the doors.

My new friends helped me understand that my false comfort of alcohol was an idol and how to surrender it to God. I got through a whole day without drinking. Then another and another. A month. A year. A decade. I was a miracle too!

Now, I help people get through their piles of rubble and watch them become miracles. God has used me to help bring hope and healing to others.

In the recovery community, some don't make it, but there are also millions of walking miracles. God works miracles in so many ways: through creation, healings, supernatural intervention, and dramatic life change. I am a life-changing miracle.

Between my sobriety date and the present, I have accumulated a lot more wreckage. I have learned to be at peace with my troubled path because my testimony helps others in areas where I was previously unqualified. I'm not saying God wanted me to make those mistakes and go through painful experiences, but he can ultimately use all of it to benefit others.

A cool perspective is that I can walk through the grocery store, restaurant, mall, or anywhere and know other miracles are walking nearby. As I pass homeless people on the corner, I can pray that they will soon be one of the miracles too.

And God confirmed the message by giving signs and wonders and various miracles and gifts of the Holy Spirit whenever he chose.
Hebrews 2:4 NLT

Lord, you are a miracle-working God! Thank you for the miracles you are about to do in the lives of these readers. Help them see the next right step clearly and encourage them as they venture into unknown territory and do uncomfortable things. *~Amen.*

Chapter 41

Gatekeepers

Now when the wall was rebuilt and I had installed the doors, and the gatekeepers, the singers, and the Levites were appointed.
Nehemiah 7:1

The rhythm of a city in Nehemiah's time was tied to the rising and setting of the sun and the opening and closing of the gates. Once the walls were completed, Jerusalem could close the gates each night, and the people could sleep safely. Regular routines could also be re-established with the wall finished and gatekeepers on duty.

With the construction complete, the people needed to start assuming the responsibilities of daily living again. Nehemiah could also begin restoring the temple activities. As his first order of business, he set up the worship teams and appointed the priests for their functions.

The other significant appointments included gatekeepers. These trustworthy guards handled community safety and protected their economic activity. The families, businesspeople, purveyors, and travelers could come and go during the daylight hours, and a gatekeeper always knew what was happening. The gatekeepers kept track of who came in and out. They were always on the lookout for undesirables and troublemakers.

Nehemiah mentioned that the wall had ten gates. Each gate served as a way in and out of the city, with some gates having specific purposes, such as the Fish Gate, where fishermen entered and exited. The Dung gate was for disposing of—you guessed it, undesirable waste. Sometimes, garbage must exit the city, but the most crucial job of the gatekeeper is to keep unwanted junk out.

In the Bible, gates and doors are often used metaphorically to refer to protection mechanisms for our hearts. We need to guard our hearts. We must be wise gatekeepers concerning what we allow to come in and out of our lives. We must be wise because undesirable junk will try to invade our sphere. In John 10, Jesus talks about the thief coming to steal, kill, and destroy. He uses a great illustration: The enemy will hop the fence or find a hole to sneak in when we aren't expecting it. Obviously, Jesus is talking about Satan and his demonic team of evil spirits as the thief who wants to come in and steal us away from our Good Shepherd, Jesus.

When we open the doors of our vulnerable places to the enemy, we give him the right to harass us. Our eyes and ears are examples of the gates or doors into our souls. So, it follows that hearing and watching violence, porn, etc., opens the gates wide for demonic harassment. Our willful participation in sinful practices opens doors, especially activities related to the occult, new age, porn, witchcraft, or false religions.

Harassment can be in the form of temptations, addictions, relationship problems, fears, sicknesses, infirmities, mental fogginess, disorders, and more. As we have already discussed, most agree that as Christians, we cannot be *possessed* by the demonic, but we definitely can be *harassed* in our soul (mind, will, emotions) and body. With the power and authority of Jesus Christ, who already lives in all believers, we can evict demonic oppressors and close off their access forever. This process is called deliverance.

I have been through several inner healing and deliverance sessions on my journey. Inner healing is the process of dismantling negative stronghold thinking patterns so we can renew our minds. We've talked a lot about those steps already. In deliverance, we eliminate the influence of evil spirits, just like Jesus and the disciples did. It's not a weird or spooky process. Deliverance is part of the Great Commission (Mark 16:17) and part of the definition of the original word for salvation. The Greek word[1] used in the New Testament for salvation is *sozo*, which has multiple definitions that can be translated into English as "saved, healed, protected, delivered, or made whole." We need both inner healing and deliverance because, as the saying goes, you can't cast out a stronghold, and you can't counsel a demon.

An example of how deliverance helps bring freedom was a ministry session I had about a year before writing this book. The Holy Spirit unexpectedly showed me an area that needed work. I suddenly said a name I had not thought about for years. This name represented some evil abuse I had already forgiven. I had purposefully put the name out of my mind because the inner healing part was already done. But after I said the name, I realized its significance. Although I had already forgiven the abuse, this demonic part was never addressed. After casting out the spirit associated with the name, I repented for allowing it in. Then, I asked the Holy Spirit to close that door and experienced one of the most significant breakthroughs of my entire healing process. I didn't growl, vomit, or writhe on the floor. We just commanded it to leave forever, and I found great freedom and peace. This may be controversial, but it was authentic, powerful, and a major step forward for me. Deep wounds were healed by pulling out this evil root, resulting in immense peace. That gate was now completely closed.

Building a path to freedom involves many small victories and an occasional monumental breakthrough. Hearing God's voice is a key. Sensitivity to what he is saying helps us manage the gates to our hearts. Jesus constantly prompts us to make the right choice, but we don't always listen. Sometimes, our desires outweigh our wisdom. Even then, we still have a path to return to safety.

Very truly I tell you Pharisees, anyone who does not enter the sheep pen by the gate, but climbs in by some other way, is a thief and a robber. The one who enters by the gate is the shepherd of the sheep. The gatekeeper opens the gate for him, and the sheep listen to his voice. He calls his own sheep by name and leads them out.
John 10:1–3 NIV

Jesus, you taught us about the dangers of mismanaging the gates to our hearts. Even when we have let the enemy in, you still call us by name and offer a way back to safety. I'm praying for every reader who needs to shut out the enemy, Lord, that they hear your voice. You are the safe shepherd and gatekeeper. *~Amen.*

Chapter 42

Trusted

I put Hanani my brother, and Hananiah the commander of the citadel, in
charge of Jerusalem, for he was a faithful man and
feared God more than many.
Nehemiah 7:2

After the wall was finished, it was time to set up the city operations. As anyone would, Nehemiah wanted people he trusted to be
the new leaders. One such person was his brother, who had shown
concern for Jerusalem all along. Nehemiah also trusted a man
named Hananiah because of his faith. These two men had shown
the kind of integrity needed to help govern the city. They cared
about God and provided a trustworthy filter for decision-making.
When choosing leaders, we want to surround ourselves with qualified people who share our fundamental values, as well as those
with wisdom and varied backgrounds.

Gold is beautiful, but on its own, it is weak and needs to be
mixed with other metals for strength and durability so that it can
be trusted to hold up during daily use. The same goes for leaders.
Nehemiah started by building a team with two individuals who
could hold one another up, cover each other's blind spots, and
develop solid governing plans. This team demonstrated accountability and dependability because they trusted each other.

Trust. All of us struggle to trust others after a challenging experience. Breakups, trauma, rejection, betrayal, layoffs, or bad financial deals are examples of situations that can wreck our ability to trust others. And a hurtful church experience leaves us without a foundation. Since all these traumas happened to me simultaneously, I strived to discern where to place my trust. People are not always what we think they are, leaving us to process hurt so we can emerge on the other side with victory. We need to learn how to trust again. The enemy wins that battle whenever we don't address our hurts and disappointments.

The events that crushed me also helped me learn valuable lessons about how to trust, wait for the unfolding of truth, and process disappointments. After I overcame the life-shattering events I shared in this book, many smaller events shook me and taught me new lessons about trust. A death, a betrayal, a lie, workplace politics, a promise broken, hopeful relationships, and even pandemic policies and political extremes—these have kept me in cycles of grief and joy in diverse ways. Did these experiences change how I trust people and the systems of the world? Yes, they did. These shakings have all happened to me in the past several years, and maybe to you too.

Think about that list again, but this time a little more carefully: death, betrayal, lies, workplace drama, family politics, promises broken, hopeful relationships, the outcomes of our pandemic, and political extremes. Such events are just part of living. Our spiritual maturity develops as we learn to process them, so we don't emerge with fear, bitterness, or unforgiveness.

Here are some ways to process those events. Think of an emotional turmoil you experienced recently and ask yourself:

- How far did my emotions spike when that happened?

- Where was my trust along the way? In myself, others, or God?

- Am I still angry at someone, including God or myself?

- What did I learn as a principle?

- Have I formed any new stronghold thinking or vows as a result?

  - That includes beliefs that say I will *always* or *never* do something again.

  - Can I change that stronghold into a healthy boundary instead?

- What should I trust going forward?

  - Am I building my road to freedom by trusting God or building a new wall by trusting myself?

Jesus reminds us that we will have periods of grief, but they are temporary, and joy will follow. Even though he told the disciples this less than twenty-four hours before his death, they didn't understand the depth of the teaching until after the resurrection and the outpouring of the Holy Spirit. Until the plan of God unfolded, Jesus' death was upsetting and confusing. But when the whole picture developed, his death became undeniably, outrageously spectacular.

That's how it is with our road to freedom. That road is paved with bricks representing broken trusts, our grief, and pain, but the destination takes us to a place of joy if we trust in the right people: God, Jesus, and our friend, the Holy Spirit.

So with you: Now is your time of grief, but I will see you again and you will rejoice, and no one will take away your joy. In that day you will no longer ask me anything. Very truly I tell you, my Father will give you whatever you ask in my name. Until now you have not asked for anything in my name. Ask and you will receive, and your joy will be complete.
John 16:22–24 NIV

Thank you, Jesus, that when we trust in you, no one can steal our joy—unless we give it to them. For anyone who gave their joy away, I pray now for joy to be restored. *~In the mighty name of Jesus! Amen.*

Chapter 43

Culture of Rubble

Now the city was large and spacious, but there were few people in it,
and the houses had not yet been rebuilt. So my God put it into my
heart to assemble the nobles, the officials and the common people for
registration by families. I found the genealogical record of those who had
been the first to return... The whole company numbered 42,360.
Nehemiah 7:4–5, 66 NIV

When Babylonian King Nebuchadnezzar invaded Jerusalem, he destroyed the wall, the temple, and the homes. He captured the people and transported them to Persia to be assimilated into his culture. When the political relationships improved, many people returned and settled in their homeland, but Jerusalem was still a run-down city. Now that the wall was finished, Nehemiah could assemble the people to start a new season of national unity.

This group of Israelites had been back in their land for several years yet had left it in a state of destruction. They had lost their culture while captives in Babylon and never recovered the traditions of their ancestors or developed a love for their homeland. They were blind to the rubble they lived in and accepted the destruction as normal.

They still lived in the culture of rubble.

The next phase of Nehemiah's leadership would be to help his people rediscover the nation they were called to be. After the great accomplishment of rebuilding the wall, the people could see their capabilities as a nation. They would discover they were home, and the time had come to live like it.

I was progressing reasonably well, building my path to freedom, when I noticed I still saw myself as a victim. When meeting new people, I would summarize my life with tragedies instead of victories. Although I was doing all the right things I had learned, I still clung to an identity that wanted sympathy.

There is a fundamental spiritual principle of sowing and reaping. Actually, it is a spiritual *law.* This law is active for everyone, Christian or not. Some call it karma. What you sow, you reap. What you plant, you will harvest. If you sow rubble, you will reap rubble. If you sow change and freedom (like we see Nehemiah doing), you will reap change and freedom.

The law of sowing and reaping tells me that if I operate with fear-filled decisions, I will develop a fear-motivated personality that ignores many wise options. If I embrace victim thinking, then I will view the world through a lens where I am already defeated. My fruit will be bitterness and resentment when unforgiveness resides in my heart. It feels completely normal to pursue wrong attitudes because they come naturally after life crumbles. Rather than the fruit that comes with negativity, I want the fruit of a prosperous and joyful life. I must sow the right seed to get the fruit I want, but it's hard to sow smiles when you're still crawling out of the pit of despair.

I *was* a victim, so what was wrong with admitting that? The problem is not acknowledging the facts but *embracing* them as my permanent lot in life. I made victimhood my identity so everyone would know my tale of woe and feel sorry for me. Even though I was making significant progress, I was still embracing my own culture of rubble.

Yep. I was still sowing some bad seeds along with the good seeds. I discovered that my terrible experiences planted seeds of fear, bitterness, victimization, shame, and failure that became firmly rooted. These mindsets had become strongholds that pleased my worldly nature and gave me attention that comforted me in an unhealthy way.

I should not get comfortable in the rubble because that will keep me rooted there. Change requires my willful choice, but

I need to hear the Holy Spirit nudging me. I can only be an overcomer with the help of the Holy Spirit, who pulls me out of the culture of rubble. The guidance of the Holy Spirit gives me the supernatural strength to follow through with needed changes and teaches me to sow in the Spirit.

I choose not to be a victim and will not live in a culture of rubble.

Do not be deceived: God cannot be mocked. A man reaps what he sows. Whoever sows to please their flesh, from the flesh will reap destruction; whoever sows to please the Spirit, from the Spirit will reap eternal life.
Galatians 6:7–8 NIV

Lord, you are a beautiful teacher, and I ask that you show us the lies that deceive us when we have grown comfortable with our pile of rubble. I pray that every reader sees a way to sow in the Spirit so that we can be victorious overcomers. *~Amen.*

Chapter 44

Spiritual Abuse

And all the people gathered as one person at the public square which was in front of the Water Gate, and they asked Ezra the scribe to bring the Book of the Law of Moses which the LORD had given to Israel. Then Ezra the priest brought the Law before the assembly of men, women, and all who could listen with understanding.
Nehemiah 8:1–2

The Jewish people had returned to Israel from Babylon in several waves. An official named Zerubbabel led the first group, and the second group came with a priest named Ezra. Ezra arrived in Jerusalem about ten to fifteen years before the third group, led by our hero, Nehemiah. Babylon's King Artaxerxes had commissioned Ezra to return to Jerusalem, and he was still there when Nehemiah came to town.

While the Jewish people were captives in Babylon, they lost much of their culture and heritage. The ancient practice of exiling conquered people was successful in its intent: to disconnect the captives from their heritage, dilute their customs, remove their religious beliefs, and build an allegiance to the conquering nation. This strategy conforms people to their captor's cultural norms instead of their true faith. The first few chapters of the Book of Daniel include stories about this when King Nebuchadnezzar first brought the Israelites to Babylon. A handful of faithful ones stayed loyal to God, but many bowed to Nebuchadnezzar.

Stripping people of their religious beliefs is a form of spiritual abuse that is still operating in our time and is sometimes called the spirit of Babylon or the spirit of the Antichrist.

Nehemiah and Ezra worked together to reestablish some Jewish traditions and restore the people's relationship with God. After completing the wall, Ezra, a teacher and historian, initiated the celebration by educating the people about God and their heritage. The plan was to restore the people to faith and worship that honored God—to their cultural and spiritual practices forgotten during the Babylonian captivity. Ezra acted as a bridge back to their original culture, traditions, and teachings with the books of Moses, breaking the effects of the spiritual abuse of Babylon.

My faith journey has included many phases of spiritual growth, some phases of exploding faith and some steady uphill climbs. However, this constant growth in my walk with the Lord was interrupted by spiritual abuse from multiple sources.

The most notable type of spiritual abuse we hear about is when a church leader sexually abuses someone under their care, but the problem is much broader and often more subtle than that. Any time someone uses their biblical authority or Scripture to manipulate others, it is spiritual abuse. Using Bible verses out of context can make it easy to manipulate others. Spiritual abuse also includes situations where someone forces their religious views (or lack of them) on others.

Spiritual abuse can happen within the context of families, relationships, marriage, and churches. It occurs when Bible verses, especially those that contain the word *submit*, are used to justify wrong desires, punish, or control others. Scripture can be misinterpreted and used out of context in ways that don't align with the overall teaching of the Bible. Another common kind of spiritual abuse is when church leaders misuse their position to control the decisions of members, their finances, and their life direction. I have seen leaders dictate what jobs people can have, who they can date, where they live, and other aspects of daily life and worship routines. Satan wins people to his side through spiritual abuse by threatening that God will reject them if they disobey. People end up either rejecting God altogether or viewing God as a demanding tyrant who can never be pleased.

All spiritual abuse deeply damages our souls, souls like mine. It took me to a place of great fear, confusion, and mistrust. I truly felt that God loved other people more than me because of how Scripture was used against me to punish me. I was subjected to ongoing twisting of God's Word and doctrine by my spouse and church, making me question what I knew and my good judgment. Thankfully, we have the enduring truth that God still loves us, no matter how terrible the abuse is. When we are under abuse, however, we can struggle to remember that Jesus stood in our place so that God only sees us through the righteous lens of Jesus. God isn't the bad guy.

The rebuilding process required me to stop blaming the individuals involved because people will always be flawed. My battle is not against flesh and blood but against the powers of this dark world (Ephesians 6:12). I also refuse to blame God for the choices individual people make. He allows evil to exist, and I accept that. People choose to make right or wrong choices. God never promises us a life without suffering. My response is what matters, meaning I must forgive them (but not necessarily trust them and reconcile with them).

So, I read, reread, and studied the New Testament with fresh eyes and an open heart. I listened to solid teachings, read books, attended freedom seminars, and took classes. As led by the Holy Spirit, I studied until I believed God's Word with a fresh perspective, believing his promises and principles in my heart, not just in my head. I immersed myself in God and trusted the Holy Spirit to rebuild my heart, especially my identity in Christ.

This is the covenant I will establish with the people of Israel after that time, declares the Lord. I will put my laws in their minds and write them on their hearts. I will be their God, and they will be my people.
Hebrews 8:10 NIV

Lord, the intentions of others can have such an impact on our faith. I pray for those who have been affected by spiritual abuse to seek you more diligently instead of running away. You are God. Your love will heal our hearts. Thank you for always welcoming us back to the truth of who you are. *~In Jesus' name. Amen.*

Rejoicing

Finding Joy

Brighter Freedom

Chapter 45

Listening

He read it aloud from daybreak till noon
as he faced the square before the Water Gate in the presence of the men,
women and others who could understand. And all the people listened
attentively to the Book of the Law.
Nehemiah 8:3 NIV

When you are in a crowd trying to hear a speech, you want everything around you to be quiet. You strain your ears to listen to what is being said. You try to tune out everything else and give it your full attention. That's listening attentively. Today, we have microphones and loudspeakers, but before electricity, people just had to yell when speaking publicly. The audience had to be incredibly quiet and attentive to hear every word.

This verse reminds me of the scene where Jesus taught the crowds in *The Chosen*[1]. The disciples spread out at various distances from Jesus to loudly repeat what was said so people farther away could hear the message. While I personally like to think that Jesus had supernatural amplification, this kind of verbal relay team was common in ancient times. This kind of verbal relay process may have been implemented for Nehemiah and Ezra.

Nehemiah lived in a time when people truly would listen attentively. They didn't have schedules that rushed everyone to the point of stress. They didn't carry phones that allowed them to multitask by giving attention to someone miles away instead of the person they were with. They could be more focused than we are today.

I have had listening challenges my whole life. In elementary school, I frequently got in trouble for talking in class. The words "talks too much" were on most of my report cards. As an adult in the workplace, I would stop listening to someone and interrupt as soon as I thought of (in my opinion) a better idea than theirs. I wanted to be heard more than I wanted to listen. I have been insensitive, harsh, and rude for most of my life, and those characteristics are ingrained in my old nature.

My listening skills changed a lot when I began attending recovery meetings because those groups have strict rules against interrupting. For the first time, I listened attentively to what others were saying. These meetings helped me improve my interactions with people. I still have a long way to go, but now I am better able to recognize when I'm insensitive. I probably owe amends to many people I hurt without ever realizing it.

Honoring others is a way to help adjust our listening skills. We can honor the people we are with by listening to them. We may not even respect a person, but we can still give them our attention when appropriate. Listening takes conscious effort and is a skill we can purposefully develop. To do this, we must take our eyes off ourselves and focus on the people around us.

But what about listening to what God says? That challenges us in more significant ways. The Bible tells us to listen to God's Word and to *do* what it says (James 1:22). Listening is where change begins, but it's just the start of the journey. Then, we take action. Freedom from our past comes by transforming our minds so that our hearts want to change. Hearing, then listening, then doing.

Little by little, brick by brick, our freedom path redefines the kind of person we are. As we allow God to work in us by changing our hearts, we can begin to discard old behaviors and find new kinds of joy in our lives.

Do not merely listen to the word, and so deceive yourselves.
Do what it says. Anyone who listens to the word but does not do what it
says is like someone who looks at his face in a mirror and, after looking at
himself, goes away and immediately forgets what he looks like.
But whoever looks intently into the perfect law that gives freedom, and
continues in it—not forgetting what they have heard, but doing it—they
will be blessed in what they do.
James 1:22–25 NIV

Lord, your Word says that studying your ways brings freedom. But our job is to listen. We must remember, digest, and incorporate it into the fabric of our lives. Father God, help us to love your Word and your ways more than the ways of the world around us. *~Amen.*

Chapter 46

Elevated

Ezra the teacher of the Law stood on a high wooden platform built for the occasion. Ezra opened the book. All the people could see him because he was standing above them; and as he opened it, the people all stood up.
Nehemiah 8:4–5 NIV

Ezra read the book of the law from a raised platform so the people could see and hear him better. The book of the law referred to here is known as the Torah by the Jews and is the first five books of the Christian Bible. From this elevated platform, the people began a new era of restoring important historical values that had eroded from their culture.

While in Babylonian captivity, the Jewish people forgot their knowledge of God and the great miracles he performed for them because society stopped elevating these values. The culture of Babylon took over, and their traditions faded away. Like previous cycles in Israel's history, the Jewish people had forgotten about God's word and how much he loved them. Yet each time this pattern of forgetting occurred, God raised up a champion to bring his people back to him.

Now, Ezra and Nehemiah opened the books for everyone in the community to hear. All the people stood for the reading of the word so they could rise up and honor God. They would learn about the incredible miracles God did for their ancestors and hear the old stories, teachings, and life instructions God had entrusted to their nation.

In early Jewish history, the Bible records an interesting event that involved elevation while the Jewish people wandered in the desert. The Israelites were being bitten by snakes, getting sick, and dying (Numbers 21:4–9). God instructed Moses to make a snake of bronze and lift it high on a pole for the people to see. When they looked up at the pole, the sick people were healed. This event was a foreshadowing of the redemptive cross of Jesus. Looking up to this symbol of healing brought life to those who were dying, just like looking to Jesus on the cross can bring spiritual and physical healing to us today. Jesus had to be elevated on the cross, representing our sins, so God's plan for our salvation could be completed.

Jesus told people *in advance* that he would be lifted up so we could be saved (John 3:14-17), but no one understood it until *after* it happened. In verse seventeen, he uses the same Greek word for salvation we discussed previously: sozo. Remember, it means to be saved, delivered, made whole, and healed. As we look up to Jesus, that is what happens on a spiritual level. We are saved from our sins, healed from our sicknesses and heartbreaks, and delivered from our strongholds and torments.

Jesus' words were fulfilled when he was lifted up on the cross. After that, he was elevated in the most spectacular way of all: he was raised from the dead, raised to new life. With the outpouring of the Holy Spirit, regular people have been empowered to do the kinds of miraculous things that Jesus did (John 14:12). But we can only do them by elevating Jesus. As our relationship with Jesus is elevated, we demote old priorities and start living in the kingdom of God.

Elevating Jesus to a position of lordship (as opposed to just someone we admire) is a process of changing what we love. It's a process of moving away from loving the things of the world to loving the things of heaven. For most of us, the transition is a slow process of awakening to what God wants for us and realizing that the things of this world are just bricks of rubble that weigh us down. Without removing them, we continue living in wreckage even though it feels completely normal.

As we elevate Jesus, we begin to recognize what we do without thinking. An example for me goes way back to when I was a new Christian. I didn't even think about the words that came from my mouth. Using the f-bomb was normal because I had always talked that way. Then, at thirty-two, I became a mother and saw many aspects of life differently. A new lens was added to my perspective, and I didn't want my kids to grow up hearing foul language from me, so I started paying attention to the kind of words I was using and, over time, cleaned up my language.

Some of the changes are minor, and others are significant. They are evidence of a heart that continues to elevate Jesus as Lord rather than doing whatever we want. The changes may feel unnatural and awkward until we move another brick from the old pile of wreckage to the new pathway of freedom. We can move each brick with joy and hope, not from fear or obligation.

And as Moses lifted up the serpent in the wilderness, even so must the Son of Man be lifted up, that whoever believes in Him should not perish but have eternal life.
John 3:14-15 NKJV

Jesus, we lift you up today. Your cross represents salvation, healing, and deliverance for our ongoing rebuilding process. Help us all elevate you to a place of prominence in our lives so that we keep our eyes focused on you. *~Amen.*

Chapter 47

Understanding

They read from the Book of the Law of God, making it clear and giving the
meaning so that the people understood
what was being read.
Nehemiah 8:8 NIV

When the books of the law were read to the community, a team
of mentors was available to help ensure that the people heard the
words and understood their meaning. Understanding brought new
life to everyone. That's what the Word of God does for us.

In the Bible, we learn that the Word of God is alive. Scripture
has depth and can be read with many levels of understanding.
These layers range from information all the way to personal revelation. We will obtain intellectual knowledge if we read the Word
just to get through the text. We can also read the Bible to find a
deeper insight into the nature of God and man.

Our intellectual knowledge can help us become biblically lit-
erate on a basic level, but we can always achieve more insight.
When we dig deeper, we discover other perspectives and spiritual
applications that we didn't initially realize. Knowledge is the start
of understanding.

As we have walked through the story of Nehemiah, we have
exposed concepts that may have differed from your initial understanding of a particular verse. Knowing more about world events
and the historical culture adds new insight. Knowing more about
the nature and will of God adds a different level of understanding.
Knowing more about God's slowly unraveling plan of salvation
adds yet another layer of depth. We want to grow not only in
knowledge but also in depth of understanding. The same was

true for the people of Jerusalem in our story. As they heard the Word of God for the first time, they began a new adventure in understanding God with new clarity.

In the kingdom of God, the more we seek, the more we find. The thirstier we are, the more we are refreshed.

As a young adult, I had a very wrong understanding of God. I knew God was a supernatural being who created everything, but because of my liberal upbringing, I incorrectly imposed my worldview on my understanding of God. I used excuses like "God just wants us to be happy" for my bad behavior because I figured I could define happiness myself. I rejected many godly teachings as outdated, religious thinking. The things of God seemed foolish to me. That is, until I decided to genuinely pursue God.

When I became interested in my personal relationship with Jesus, I started wanting to know what God was really like rather than the partial knowledge in my head. Those old notions were shattered as I read the Bible and learned what Jesus said instead of the assumptions I had. I began to build a foundation of genuine knowledge. Then, I added to that knowledge by digging deeper for more understanding. I became fascinated with how God's plan for salvation through Jesus was woven into history. And even more fascinating was how salvation could strengthen us to withstand the difficulties of this life.

When I was baptized in the Holy Spirit, I began a new adventure in understanding this aspect of the Trinity. Bible verses that I had read so many times before suddenly came alive in a new way. I could now understand them with the mind of Christ rather than just the mind of Cindy. I was amazed by how much brighter the light of the Holy Spirit could shine on the Word of God.

Some concepts are only spiritually discerned because we have the mind of Christ, and we can understand all things. We didn't receive part of the Holy Spirit or part of the mind of Christ. No. We got the whole package. Spiritual maturity, however, is accessing more of what we have been given. I must overcome the old me to fully walk in the newness of what I have been given. My maturity is built by shedding my soulish inclinations and allowing my spiritual nature to blossom.

But a natural person does not accept the things of the Spirit of God, for they are foolishness to him; and he cannot understand them, because they are spiritually discerned. But the one who is spiritual discerns all things, yet he himself is discerned by no one. For who has known the mind of the Lord, that he will instruct him?
But we have the mind of Christ.
1 Corinthians 2:14–16

Father God, there are many levels of understanding your Word. Thank you for helping us spiritually discern the depth of what it reveals. You have given us your Spirit. The brilliance of your mind is part of our salvation, and because of that, you help us get through the rubble and come out transformed. In the mighty name of Jesus, I come into agreement with your Word. *~Amen.*

Chapter 48

Encouragement

Then Nehemiah, who was the governor, and Ezra the priest and scribe, and the Levites who taught the people said to all the people, "This day is holy to the LORD your God; do not mourn or weep." For all the people were weeping when they heard the words of the Law.
Nehemiah 8:9

Some people have walked into a job performance review thinking they've been doing great and quite unexpectedly learned that their supervisor had a different opinion. They were not performing up to the job's expectations. It's discouraging to find out you haven't done what you should have. That's what the Jewish people were experiencing in this scenario. They began to realize that the nation had meaningful purposes and instructions, and it broke their hearts to know they weren't living up to them.

The Jewish law said that the books should be read aloud to the people once every seven years. Because they had not done that, they lost sight of their community and purpose. The cultural norms for living in Babylon had become their guidelines, but God had different expectations for his people, which caused them deep regret and mourning.

In addition to rules of conduct, the books of the law were the storehouse of stories about God's great miracles. As the people listened, they learned about God's nature and goodness, how he had chosen them to be his special people, and how to worship and honor him. As they read the law, the people became aware that they had not been living to honor God. The people, overwhelmed by realizing their wrong lifestyle, found solace in Nehemiah's words. He knew that the people needed comfort and reassurance.

Celebrations were on the horizon, but first, the people needed his words of encouragement and comfort.

Obstacles often divert us from our purpose and goals as we trudge through life. Sometimes, we don't even realize it's happening until it's too late, but other times, obvious tragedies and stresses get in our way and take us away from our intended path. And now, we even know that a pandemic can derail our plans.

We are told that we *will* have troubles in this life. We can expect seasons of grief, regret, wounding, sickness, financial hardship, and even persecution. However, as Christians, we have been given the ultimate comforter: the Holy Spirit. God himself lives in us, providing us with the comfort, power, strength, and encouragement to continue.

Even though we have the most excellent comforter living in us, we also need the comfort of real people. When I was a pile of rubble, I needed human encouragement. I was grateful for the encouragement I got from others. Later, as I healed, I began encouraging others. After a period of trials comes times of rebuilding and restoration, and then a season of serving others with the same encouragement we needed during our troubled times. It's a beautiful cycle.

We have been commissioned to share God's outpouring of love and comfort with others. Encouragement is one of the easiest ways to help others, and it doesn't take much effort to let someone know you care. I have a friend who texts a Bible verse every day to encourage others. One of my other dear friends loves to send cards in the mail when she knows I need encouragement. I treasure those and save some of them to remind myself later how blessed I am.

We need those who have overcome the impossible as guides and inspiration for others just starting their journey to being brighter and freer. The entire recovery community is built around a model of encouragement, because helping others is beautifully integrated into all twelve-step programs. The twelfth step teaches people to serve by passing on their hope and wisdom to others. This cycle of encouragement is why you hear about people who have been in recovery for years and years. You don't have to be in a twelve-step program to see this wisdom or incorporate it into your life.

Serving by encouraging others is essential in two respects. First, people buried in their rubble need help to get out. We need to know that we are not the only ones who have experienced these problems and need the encouragement of seeing other people who have achieved victory. Second, encouraging others and serving are integral parts of our faith. Encouraging others helps us find value and purpose in what we have gone through.

No matter how our pile of rubble was created or how our healing journey unfolds, we need to know that we are not alone. God is calling us to be there for each other, passing on the encouragement and comfort we have received.

He comforts us in all our troubles so that we can comfort others. When they are troubled, we will be able to give them the same comfort God has given us.
2 Corinthians 1:4 NLT

Father God, you have given us the greatest comforter of all: the Holy Spirit. He enables us to encourage and help others as they start working on their piles of rubble. Teach us to be vulnerable enough to pay it forward and encourage others. *~Amen.*

Chapter 49

Joy

And Nehemiah continued, "Go and celebrate with a feast of rich foods
and sweet drinks, and share gifts of food with people who have nothing
prepared. This is a sacred day before our Lord. Don't be dejected and sad,
for the joy of the LORD is your strength!"
Nehemiah 8:10 NLT

The people were moved to tears after hearing the books of the law
read to them, but they were about to begin celebrating a holiday
of feasting, so Nehemiah told them to wipe away their tears. He
knew the lessons produced a deep joy for the soul. This joy carries
you through difficulties and disasters, giving you the strength to
face anything.

The above Bible verse, "The joy of the Lord is your strength,"
is familiar to many of us. I even have a sign with that Scripture
in my kitchen. Let's dig in and learn a little more from *Strong's
Exhaustive Concordance of the Bible*.

- **Joy**: The original Hebrew word[1] for *joy* can also be translated as *rejoicing* or *gladness*. I love the definition used in
  the New Testament where the Greek word[2] often used for
  joy, like in the fruit of the Spirit (Galatians 5:22)) means
  "cheerfulness:" or "*a calm delight*." As I started to understand joy, this was a safe and easy place for me to begin.

- **Strength**: Here is where it gets good. This word in the
  original Hebrew[3] is defined as a "fortified place; figura-
  tively a *defense*: force, fort (-ress), rock, strength." In the
  context of a story about building a wall of safety around a

city, this definition shines a new light on *strength*.

Take a look at Nehemiah's most famous line with this fresh context by replacing it with those definitions:

The calm delight of the Lord is your defense.

Wow! Walls can protect cities, but the joy of the Lord can protect your heart. Fortifying ourselves in God's calm delight can be our defense mechanism—our fortified place where we are not easily offended, wounded, or broken.

Thanks, Nehemiah, for a new perspective.

Today, we live in a society that strives for happiness, but I have come to a point where I strive for joy instead—specifically, calm delight.

"Joy as your strength" is often discussed by comparing joy and happiness. Circumstances may deliver happiness, while joy can sustain you *through* circumstances. Because happiness fades quickly, we need a continuous flow of positive external events to stay happy. Joy, however, produces satisfaction that transcends what may be going on around us.

The kind of joy referred to in the Bible is more like an underlying attitude that is not affected by external events. Biblical joy is a characteristic rather than a feeling; it gives peace to withstand the storms of life that come to us all. This kind of joy is enduring and constant. That's why it can be our strength and defense.

After years of darkness, I was discouraged and longed for the happiness I had experienced many years ago. I looked back at the happy family I had while my kids were young. Later, after I finally quit drinking, I was making great friends in my Christian recovery group. I was passionate about my work. I had a purpose and was hopeful about the future. I was happy. Then, happiness was suddenly snatched away, and the dark years began.

As I finally started digging myself out of the rubble, I longed for the feelings of happiness I remembered. But even my happy memories were missing the *joy* of the Lord. So, I started to pray for more joy every day, along with all the fruit of the Spirit (Galatians 5:22–23). In my prayer time, I asked God to help me grow more in his love, joy, peace, patience, kindness, goodness, faithfulness, gentleness, and self-control.

I started to experience that joy as I truly processed my hurt and made Jesus the focus of my heart. I walked more with the Spirit, which felt like it helped heal my wounded soul. Since then, I've been trying to maintain that joy. Joy doesn't always look or feel like happiness, but for me, it feels satisfying, strong, safe, and content. There is more to come in my journey for joy, and I welcome God's expansion in my life.

And the disciples were continually filled
with joy and with the Holy Spirit.
Acts 13:52

Father God, we want to be continually filled with you and your joy. Thank you for the freedom that comes from your Spirit in us. Thank you for developing the fruit of the Spirit that makes us more like Jesus: love, joy, peace, patience, kindness, goodness, faithfulness, gentleness, and self-control. *~Amen.*

Chapter 50

Next Steps

So the people went away to eat and drink at a festive meal, to share gifts of food, and to celebrate with great joy because they had heard God's words and understood them.
Nehemiah 8:12 NLT

Jerusalem's people had undergone many significant transitions in just a few months. Starting with vast piles of rubble around them, they persevered through significant trials during the rebuilding process. Their success in completing the job led to great rejoicing and the renewal of God's Word in their hearts. The foundation of fresh understanding about themselves as a nation—their identity, their origins, and their testimony—brought the people to tears.

Rebuilding the walls of Jerusalem led to a significant pivot for the people of Israel as the whole nation received an identity adjustment. They were transitioning from the mindset of captives barely released from foreign exile to the understanding that they were God's chosen and beloved people.

Throughout Israel's history, they cycled between periods of loving the true God and serving the worldly gods of perversion and power. They didn't know what lessons they were missing because they lost that knowledge during their exile in Babylon. Now, they saw how God factored into every aspect of their lives, including working, parenting, eating, economics, health, politics, education, and interactions. God even had much to teach them about celebrating and enjoying festivals.

This day marked a transition for all of Israel. Now that they understood the Word of God, they turned back to him for the next steps in their national destiny, and they were glad to do it. Their destiny included descendants who would produce the Messiah of the world.

As I began digging out of my rubble, several encouraging prophetic words were spoken over me. These words confirmed that I had a heart for Freedom Ministry—the Isaiah 61 ministry of Jesus to set the captives free and comfort the brokenhearted, especially regarding addiction and recovery. The words also confirmed that books were "locked up inside of me, and the pages in my life will be used to set the captives free." Yes!

My heart's desire is to help others through writing; this was part of me long before it was confirmed in this way. However, the words encouraged me to believe that this calling was still in my future and that my failures had not disqualified me. This encouragement was beneficial because at that point I wasn't confident about my future. As it turns out, much of what I would write about was still unfolding, and only now am I actively engaging in the work of that calling.

The dedication to my own freedom journey has finally moved me into my season of sharing. It was healing first, then serving, and now sharing what I have learned along the way. I didn't know how to get started writing, but the Lord reminded me of the short devotional on Nehemiah that I had written for a special project in the past.

Writings about Nehemiah are often focused on business or leadership, but that wasn't where my heart was. What could I possibly say now about Nehemiah? But in prayer, God kept reconfirming that the devotional would be the outline for my first book. I didn't see the plan, so he gave me a new perspective on the concept of rebuilding. Look how God turned it around!

I used that original devotional as the outline. Still, as I sat down to write every day, I had no idea where the topic would go until the Holy Spirit brought these two rebuilding projects (Nehemiah's and mine) to life in my heart. He helped me understand the words of Nehemiah in a fresh way. My next steps have included a commitment to writing, not just this book, but supporting material to go with it. I also need to research the latest technology around publishing and everything that goes with being an author in today's world.

What are your next steps?

Understanding God's Word changes you, and you are never the same! Once it grabs your heart, you want to adjust and start building that path toward more of *God's* kind of freedom. Sometimes, it is little by little, and sometimes, in leaps and bounds. The redemptive story of Jesus is written on every page of the Bible, showing us that the answer to every life issue is the same: Jesus.

As we reflect on the amazing unfolding of our understanding, we find the truth that sets us free. So, let's celebrate and plan our next steps. We can take what we have been given and joyfully share it with others so they can know the truth and be free.

Jesus said to the people who believed in him, "You are truly my disciples if you remain faithful to my teachings. And you will know the truth, and the truth will set you free."
John 8:31–32 NLT

Heavenly Father, you have unraveled your plan throughout history, allowing us to know the truth that sets us free. Help us all see the next steps to put that into action. *~In the powerful name of Jesus, Amen.*

Chapter 51

Celebrate

And they found written in the Law how the LORD had commanded through Moses that the sons of Israel were to live in booths during the feast of the seventh month... And there was very great rejoicing. He read from the Book of the Law of God daily, from the first day to the last day. And they celebrated the feast seven days, and on the eighth day there was a festive assembly in accordance with the ordinance.
Nehemiah 8:14, 17–18

As the people explored the Scriptures, they discovered how God loves celebrating. He established times for all phases of life: festivals, holidays, reverence, worship, rest, fasts, and feasts. The harvest season was to be celebrated in a distinct way.

The Feast of Booths, now called Sukkot, was established as a seven-day celebration where everyone would camp out in temporary shelters (also called tents, tabernacles, or booths). God intended this feast to commemorate the years that the Israelites wandered in the desert and had to live in temporary shelters. Spending a few days each year in similar tents would remind everyone of their miraculous deliverance out of slavery from Egypt. Even today, eating meals in outdoor booths or tents is the proper way to celebrate this festival. The Feast of Booths is also a time of thanksgiving—it commemorates freedom from spending decades in the wilderness, which is undoubtedly a reason to be thankful.

The book of Exodus records that God brought the Israelites out of Egyptian slavery using miracle after miracle. However, even after having every basic need provided for them by God's miracles, the people still grumbled, and many still longed for the food and stability they had as enslaved people. Because they complained, they spent forty years in the wilderness to remove the slavery mindset of the generation that had lived in Egypt. Only then were they allowed to enter the Promised Land. While they wandered in the wilderness, God provided for their needs so they would learn to trust him. We can see the symbolism that God is our shelter in the wilderness, but he wants us to progress from the wilderness and settle in the Promised Land.

After learning about this particular feast, Nehemiah, Ezra, and all of Israel celebrated the blessings God had provided and looked ahead to his promises.

God brought me out of the wilderness, and I celebrate the date every year. When I share my recovery testimony, I compare the time when I was drinking to slavery in Egypt. Then, the times I tried to quit drinking on my own were like a season of wandering in the desert, waiting for the miracle to happen that would suddenly transport me into the promised land of sobriety. The slavery of alcoholism crept up on me. I was a Christian who slowly, over time, fell into habitual drinking. Some will say I probably was not a true Christian, but I'm sure I was, and remorse for my sinful behavior was evidence. I would sit on my couch crying out to God, asking, "Why can't I be an overcomer the way you say I am?" I now know the reason. I wanted a miracle to change me instantly, but God wanted to do it *with* me rather than *for* me.

In my heart, I didn't want to quit drinking. I just wanted the ability to drink moderately like other people. It took many years of wandering in the wilderness to change my mindset enough to see that I had to commit to long-term sobriety. The wilderness is intended to be temporary and can produce a shift from victim to God-follower. I was ready to cross the Jordan when I shifted my desire from false comforts to God alone.

When I visited Israel, I saw the Jordan River with my own eyes. Today, it is a dirty river full of hungry catfish. They have a nice area to baptize people with fences to keep out the fish, but the murky river beyond the fence is teeming with catfish waiting to nibble on anything in the water. I visualize trying to cross the river myself, but I know I won't make it. The attacks would be more than I could bear. I could only cross the river with God's miraculous provision, which he gave when I surrendered and trusted his way. I could only cross the metaphorical river of alcoholism when I was done entirely with my mentality of wandering in the wilderness and ready to partner with God to do it his way.

God wanted me to be refined like gold. Refining takes time and processing. It purges the impurities and produces a better result than the initial product. Moving into the promised land is a refining process. Enemies were in the land, so after crossing the river, the Israelites had to eliminate them and purify the places they would inhabit. Their first victory was in Jericho (Joshua 6), showing how relying entirely on God would bring success. Their second battle, in the town of Ai (Joshua 7), showed the disastrous results that can occur from acting without God's blessing.

Rather than eliminating our enemies, Jesus brought a helper to walk with us: the Holy Spirit. With the Holy Spirit, Jesus enables his followers to be overcomers. Jesus will come back someday and destroy every evil thing, but for now, our battle is to walk in our true identity and transform our mindset.

Winning these battles is worth celebrating. When we overcome a difficulty, we should commemorate it. Celebrate your salvation. Celebrate your commitment to freedom. Celebrate the day you finally said no to an addictive behavior. Celebrate the day you overcame bitterness toward your ex. Celebrate the day you broke the generational cycle and stopped being codependent. Celebrate the day you finally forgave yourself and stopped hating yourself. The Holy Spirit rejoices with you.

When Jesus was celebrating the Feast of Booths, he prophesied about the coming of the Holy Spirit which would be given to all believers. The Holy Spirit is a spiritual spring of refreshment to our thirsty souls. He is the power, and authority, and wisdom, and peace, and comfort, and truth that helps us through the battles. With the Holy Spirit in us, we can be thankful for the wilderness, the battles, the victories, the freedom, and the peace. We can celebrate the spiritual river that flows through us and never runs dry. Nothing is more significant in any religion than having the Holy Spirit live in us, and *that* is worth celebrating. Celebrate having a Spirit-filled life.

On the last and greatest day of the festival, Jesus stood and said in a loud voice, "Let anyone who is thirsty come to me and drink. Whoever believes in me, as Scripture has said, rivers of living water will flow from within them." By this he meant the Spirit, whom those who believed in him were later to receive. Up to that time the Spirit had not been given, since Jesus had not yet been glorified.
John 7:37–39 NIV

Heavenly Father, I gladly receive your precious Spirit. Holy Spirit. Fill me, flow through me, overflow in me every day like a river of living water. Please help me use every spiritual gift to work in me and bring about your purposes for my life. *~In the name of Jesus Christ, my Lord, I pray. Amen*

Chapter 52

Brighter

At the dedication of the wall of Jerusalem, the Levites were sought out
from where they lived and were brought to Jerusalem to celebrate joyfully the dedication with songs of thanksgiving and with the music of
cymbals, harps, and lyres. And on that day they offered great sacrifices,
rejoicing because God had given them great joy.
The women and children also rejoiced...
The sound of rejoicing in Jerusalem could be heard far away.
Nehemiah 12:27, 43 NIV

They had a parade, a beautiful celebration, with singers and
dancers. They went around the whole city; some paraded along
the top of the wall, and others danced on the ground. They held
grand processions with musicians and choirs singing songs of
praise and thanksgiving.

What a transformation! This story began with a town of people
who lived with an attitude of defeat. They were used to dusty piles
of rubble. Thankfully, Nehemiah, their champion, had a better
idea. He gave the people vision and encouragement to rally together and undertake an ambitious project that helped everyone.

- They learned how to work as a team.

- They protected each other.

- They worked through their problems together.

- They realigned their identity as a community.

- They were vulnerable and cried together.

- They celebrated together.

- They were thankful for what was accomplished.

The people of Israel rejoiced at the transformation.
The city was transformed, and God got the glory.
The people were transformed because the glory of God got *them*.

While working on this book, a friend asked me why I titled the book Brighter Freedom. All I could say at the time was that God gave me the title long before I started writing. I bought the domain brighterfreedom.com after doing my first freedom program — five years before I started writing. I knew Brighter Freedom would be the name of my first book, even though I had no other clue of what it would be about.

More than ten years ago, my brother had a small side business using the word *brighter* in its name. I liked it so much that I adopted the word and wove it into my life. I use it in my own business name, email addresses, profile names, and license plates. *Brighter* became my favorite word. Many of us choose a word of the year but *brighter* has been the word of my life.

Buy why? I like the idea of being a light to others, but there must be something more. Why have I been so drawn to this word? I asked the Holy Spirit to show me why my word is *brighter*. Why is it so special to me?

The following week, a specific, unrelated Bible verse kept coming up: Zephaniah 3:17. I heard the verse in multiple sermons, teachings, and even in a conversation. It was nagging at me, so I decided to look at it more closely.

The LORD your God is with you, the Mighty Warrior who saves. He will take great delight in you; in his love he will no longer rebuke you, but will rejoice over you with singing.
Zephaniah 3:17 NIV

I needed to investigate why I kept hearing this verse, so I reread the book of Zephaniah. I studied this specific verse and looked at it in several different translations. The context is about Israel being restored after a period of disobedience and their joy returning. Just like me! When my priorities shifted away from God, my actions brought devastating consequences; however, now my actions are reestablishing joy in my life.

I dug deeper. Since it's an Old Testament verse, I looked up the meaning of all the Hebrew words in *Strong's Exhaustive Concordance of the Bible*, and that's where I found the key I was looking for. I was so surprised by what I learned:

> The Hebrew definition of ***rejoice*** (H7797[1]) "A primitive root; ***to be bright***, that is, cheerful: - be glad, greatly, joy, make mirth, rejoice." (emphasis added).

Wow! That is an incredible discovery. ***To be bright!*** I was so excited! Of course, that made me want to look up the word for rejoice in Nehemiah 12:43, our chapter fifty-two verse. Guess what? This verse uses a different Hebrew word for *rejoicing* (H8055[2]), but it also means to "***brighten up***." Other words in the definition include "to cheer up, be glad, joyful, and merry."

Wow! Rejoicing is a **brightening up** for us! That was a beautiful connection for me that made the whole book come together beautifully in an unexpected way! Rejoicing brightens us!

Since *brighter* has been the word of my life, I have now adopted Zephaniah 3:17 as my life verse.

I now see how God pulled together many threads of my life. I see how He is with me and is rejoicing over me, making me brighter and giving me joy. I am filled with his love to the point that I can be comforted even in my troubles. Knowing God loves me and delights in me brings joy. He even rejoices over me like I rejoice over him.

He rejoices over YOU! He brightens us! This is freedom!

> **Now the Lord is the Spirit,**
> **and where the Spirit of the Lord is,**
> **there is freedom.**
> **2 Corinthians 3:17**

Dear Lord, as my new friends go through their own freedom journey, I pray that they will experience your love, your delight, your calm, and most of all, your freedom. Thank you for revealing the brightness of your joy to us. *~Amen and amen.*

The End Is a Beginning

Remember me for this, my God, and do not blot out what I have so faithfully done for the house of my God and its services.
Nehemiah 13:14

I still wrestle with many areas of my life, but that doesn't mean I can't move forward as a champion in my areas of success. I want to continue building my path of wholeness and freedom. I will adjust and build as long as I live, but I won't give up.

Freedom is for all of us. No matter how difficult life has been, there is a path to freedom. No matter how sinful, God continues to love you. No matter how broken, God will help rebuild. There is freedom, no matter how old we are, no matter how alone we are, no matter how bound we are.

Now may the God of hope
fill you with all joy and peace in believing,
so that you will abound in hope by the power of the Holy Spirit.
Romans 15:13

Father God, my prayer for all the readers is that they will be filled with joy, peace, and hope by the power of the Holy Spirit. You, God, are the provider of everything we need. Bless these readers with brighter freedom as they rebuild. *~In the mighty name of Jesus. Amen.*

With Love,
~Cindy

Epilogue: Love

My years of healing and rebuilding have profoundly transformed my relationship with God, with others, and myself. My understanding of God blossomed beautifully. The insight I received from the Holy Spirit has opened my spiritual eyes to see with greater depth and significance what was always there. Walking with the Lord should include partnering with every aspect of who he is. I partner with Father God. I partner with Jesus, the Son and Savior. I partner with the Holy Spirit, my helper. I partner with God in awe and respect and, most of all, in love. Love was where I found my most significant breakthrough.

Gaining an understanding of love has transformed my wounded soul. That understanding has helped set me free in many of the areas I have discussed in this book, as well as others.

I have wrestled with learning about love because I have failed miserably in this area. I felt rejected by the men who were supposed to love me, starting with my father. When our love wounds start with our daddy, we struggle to fully understand the depth of Father God's love for us. That multiplies with rejections from significant relationships. The result was that I never felt loved, even by God.

During my healing process, I became brave enough to undertake a deeper, more personal study of love in the Bible, to try filling the big hole in my heart. Well, maybe a huge hole. To fill the *ginormous* hole in my heart. Not surprisingly, one takeaway came from the great love chapter, which says:

Love is patient, love is kind. It does not envy, it does not boast, it is not proud. It does not dishonor others, it is not self-seeking, it is not easily angered, it keeps no record of wrongs. Love does not delight in evil but rejoices with the truth. It always protects, always trusts, always hopes, always perseveres. Love never fails.
1 Corinthians 13:4–8 NIV

Because this chapter is often read at weddings, many think it describes how our marriage-type love should work. In fact, I have used 1 Corinthians 13 to look at a spouse and think, "He isn't like that with me," proving that he doesn't love me. So, I needed to take a fresh look at the Bible's famous love chapter.

What if you substitute the word "love" with "God"? God is patient. God is kind. God always protects, and so forth. It gives me a different perspective. What if you substitute the word "love" with "Jesus"? Jesus is not self-seeking. Jesus does not keep a record of wrongs, and so on. And then, what if you substitute the word "love" with "Cindy"? Ouch.

I concluded that to be more like Jesus, I must be more like the love described here. I had to stop imposing these characteristics on others and start imposing them on myself.

I have learned to show love *first* so I can see others through God's perspective. I continue to study what the Bible says about love. I listen to sermons and teachings about love. I surround myself with people who model love, God's kind of love. And most importantly, I take time just to sit and soak in God's love for me. This is transformational and is not a waste of time. God's love transforms us, and I am living proof.

Finally, I could rejoice in my journey. Knowing I am loved made all the difference. It brightened me. It helped me rejoice over the process. This is the essence of freedom: knowing we are loved, knowing it deep in our souls. When we know we are loved, we can rejoice. When we rejoice, we become a brighter light along the pathway to freedom. Knowing we are loved is a truth that sets us free.

I pray that out of his glorious riches he may strengthen you
with power through his Spirit in your inner being,
so that Christ may dwell in your hearts through faith.
And I pray that you, being rooted and established in love,
may have power, together with all the Lord's holy people,
to grasp how wide and long and high and deep is the love of Christ,
and to know this love that surpasses knowledge—
that you may be filled to the measure of all the fullness of God.
Ephesians 3:16–19 NIV

Oh, God! Thank you for loving us. We need it. Our hearts crave the knowledge that we are loved. Your spirit brings love into our very being and gives us freedom—your kind of freedom. As we rejoice in you, we become the brighter version of who you created us to be. This is the freedom only found through being rooted in love *~Amen and amen.*

With Love,

~Cindy

Declarations

Renew Your Mind

We hear a lot of lies from the world around us that say we are not good enough. This is especially damaging and confusing when it comes from people who are supposed to love us. When we hear something repeatedly, we begin to believe it. To counter this, we can personalize and speak the truth of what God says about us. If we say these truths out loud, over and over, we will eventually believe them and counter those lies. It takes repetition, but this is one of the ways we can renew our minds. God uses the science of brain neuroplasticity to rewire our thought patterns!

These are Bible verses that have been paraphrased and personalized to use as declarations!

Knowing what God says about you helps heal your soul!

Declaring what God says about you is a way to renew your mind!

You can even build your own custom list like this from bible verses that speak life to your soul.

It is important to say declarations **out loud** every day. It also helps to do this whenever you are triggered, stressed, distracted, or upset.

Write your name on the blank line.

Who Am I?

I am _____, loved by Jesus (John 15:9)

I am chosen by God Himself (1Thessalonians 1:4)
I am a temple filled with his Holy Spirit (1Corinthians 3:16)
I am a child of God (John 1:12)
I am victorious in my fight against evil (Psalm 20:6)
I am an overcomer (1John 5:4)
I am free (Galatians 5:1)
I have been given joy for my strength (Nehemiah 8:10)
My sorrows will turn into joy (Jeremiah 31:13)
and my joy will be complete (John 15:11)
God almighty is my hope and my anchor (Hebrews 6:19)
He has called me by name (Isaiah 43:1)
I will not fear (Psalm 23:4)
No weapon formed against me will prevail (Isaiah 54:17)
I am more than a conqueror (Romans 8:37)
The one who is in me is
greater than the one who is in the world (1John 4:4)
I have the mind of Christ (1Corinthians 2:16)
Jesus is:
my provider (Acts 14:17)
my redeemer (Galatians 3:13)
my healer (1Peter 2:24)
my protector (Psalm 91:14)
and my friend (John 15:15)
I am forgiven and made clean (1John 1:9)
I can do all things through Christ who strengthens me (Phil 4:13)
I am not alone (Isaiah 41:10)

Thank You, Jesus. I love you, Lord.

Resources

Resources available at:
www.brighterfreedom.com

If you are blessed by this book,
please leave a review on Amazon!

Endnotes

Introductions

1. Wikipedia, "Nebuchadnezzar II," last modified September 21, 2024, at 11:30 (UTC), https://en.wikipedia.org/wiki/Nebuchadnezzar_II

2. Wikipedia, "Nehemiah," last modified August 12, 2024, at 20:02 (UTC), https://en.wikipedia.org/wiki/Nehemiah.

More, Please!

1. "Fact: How long was the journey from Babylon to Jerusalem?," ESV.org, accessed October 3, 2024, https://www.esv.org/resources/esv-global-study-bible/facts-ezra-7.

Anger, Offense and Forgiveness

1. James Strong, *Strong's Exhaustive Concordance of the Bible*, "4625. skandalon,"accessed October 3, 2024, https://biblehub.com/greek/4625.htm.

Lies

1. The 5 Love Languages, accessed October 3, 2024,https://5lovelanguages.com/.

Blessings and Curses

1. *Oxford English Dictionary*, "curse," accessed October 3, 2024, https://www.oed.com/search/dictionary/?scope=Entries&q=curse.

Vulnerable Places

1. John Loren Sandford and Mark Sandford, *Deliverance and Inner Healing* (Baker Publishing Group, 2008), 63, Kindle.

Strongholds

1. Dr. Caroline Leaf, *Switch On Your Brain: The Key to Peak Happiness, Thinking, and Health*(Baker Publishing Group, 2005), Kindle.

Devoted

1. Encyclopedia.com, "devote," last updated May 23, 2018, https://www.encyclopedia.com/literature-and-arts/language-linguistics-and-literary-terms/english-vocabulary-d/devote.

Gatekeepers

1. James Strong, *Strong's Exhaustive Concordance of the Bible*, "4982. sózó," accessed October 3, 2024, https://biblehub.com/greek/4982.htm.

Listening

1. Dallas Jenkins, "The Chosen, Season 3, Episode 8," April 9, 2023, watch.thechosen.tv/.

Joy

1. James Strong, *Strong's Exhaustive Concordance of the Bible*, "2304. chedvah," accessed October 3, 2024, https://biblehub.com/hebrew/2304.htm.

2. James Strong, *Strong's Exhaustive Concordance of the Bible*, "5479. chara," accessed October 3, 2024, https://biblehub.com/greek/5479.htm.

3. James Strong, *Strong's Exhaustive Concordance of the Bible*, "4581. maoz or mauz or maoz or mauz," accessed October 3, 2024, https://biblehub.com/hebrew/4581.htm.

Brighter

1. James Strong, *Strong's Exhaustive Concordance of the Bible*, "7797. sus or sis," accessed October 3, 2024, https://biblehub.com/hebrew/7797.htm.

2. James Strong, *Strong's Exhaustive Concordance of the Bible*, "8055. samach," accessed October 3, 2024, https://biblehub.com/hebrew/8055.htm.

www.ingramcontent.com/pod-product-compliance
Lightning Source LLC
Chambersburg PA
CBHW051830090426
42736CB00011B/1734